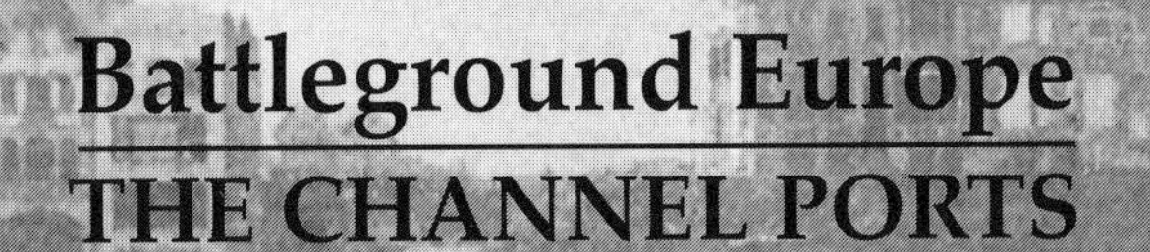

Battleground Europe

THE CHANNEL PORTS

DUNKIRK - 1940

FROM DISASTER TO DELIVERANCE

Other guides in the Second World War Battleground Europe Series:

Pegasus Bridge/Merville Battery *by* Carl Shilleto
Gold Beach *by* Christopher Dunphie & Garry Johnson
Omaha Beach *by* Tim Kilvert-Jones
Battle of the Bulge - St Vith *by* Michael Tolhurst
Calais *by* John Cooksey
March of Das Reich to Normandy *by* Philip Vickers

Battleground Europe

THE CHANNEL PORTS

DUNKIRK - 1940

FROM DISASTER TO DELIVERANCE

Patrick Wilson

LEO COOPER

COMBINED PUBLISHING
Pennsylvania

Published by
LEO COOPER
an imprint of
Pen & Sword Books Limited
47 Church Street, Barnsley, South Yorkshire S70 2AS

ISBN 0 85052 701 5

A CIP record of this book is available
from the British Library

Printed by Redwood Books Limited
Trowbridge, Wiltshire

For up-to-date information on other titles produced under the Leo Cooper imprint, please telephone or write to:
Pen & Sword Books Ltd, FREEPOST SF5, 47 Church Street
Barnsley, South Yorkshire S70 2BR
Telephone 01226 734222

Published under license in the United States of America by

COMBINED PUBLISHING

ISBN 1-58097-046-X

For information, address:
COMBINED PUBLISHING
P.O. Box 307
Conshohocken, PA 19428
E-Mail: combined@dca.net
Web: www.combinedpublishing.com
Orders: 1-800-418-6065

Cataloging in Publication Data available from the Library of Congress

CONTENTS

FOREWORD

by

MAJOR GENERAL C.A. RAMSAY, CB, OBE

The year 2000 is the 60th Anniversary of the evacuation of the British Expeditionary Force, and Allied Forces from Dunkirk. This was a classic case of improvisation based on outline contingency plans. Memories fade fast and it is timely that Patrick Wilson has produced such a detailed, eloquent and entertaining account of this epic piece of history. The background is just as important and interesting as the event.

My father's foresight, as the Naval Commander, combined with his ability to delegate and inspire people, certainly played a crucial part. Without Dunkirk, it is likely that the British Army might never have reconstituted itself sufficiently for the ultimate return to the Continent, quite apart from the political consequences that the loss of the BEF might have precipitated. It was thus fitting that my father, as Allied Naval Commander-in-Chief, was also to be in charge of Operation Neptune in June 1944.

However, the real heroes of Dunkirk were the sailors, naval and civilian, in an almost bizarre range of large and small craft, who achieved a near miracle under highly adverse conditions and many of whom were lost. The memory of all these people stands high.

Charles Ramsay

December 1999

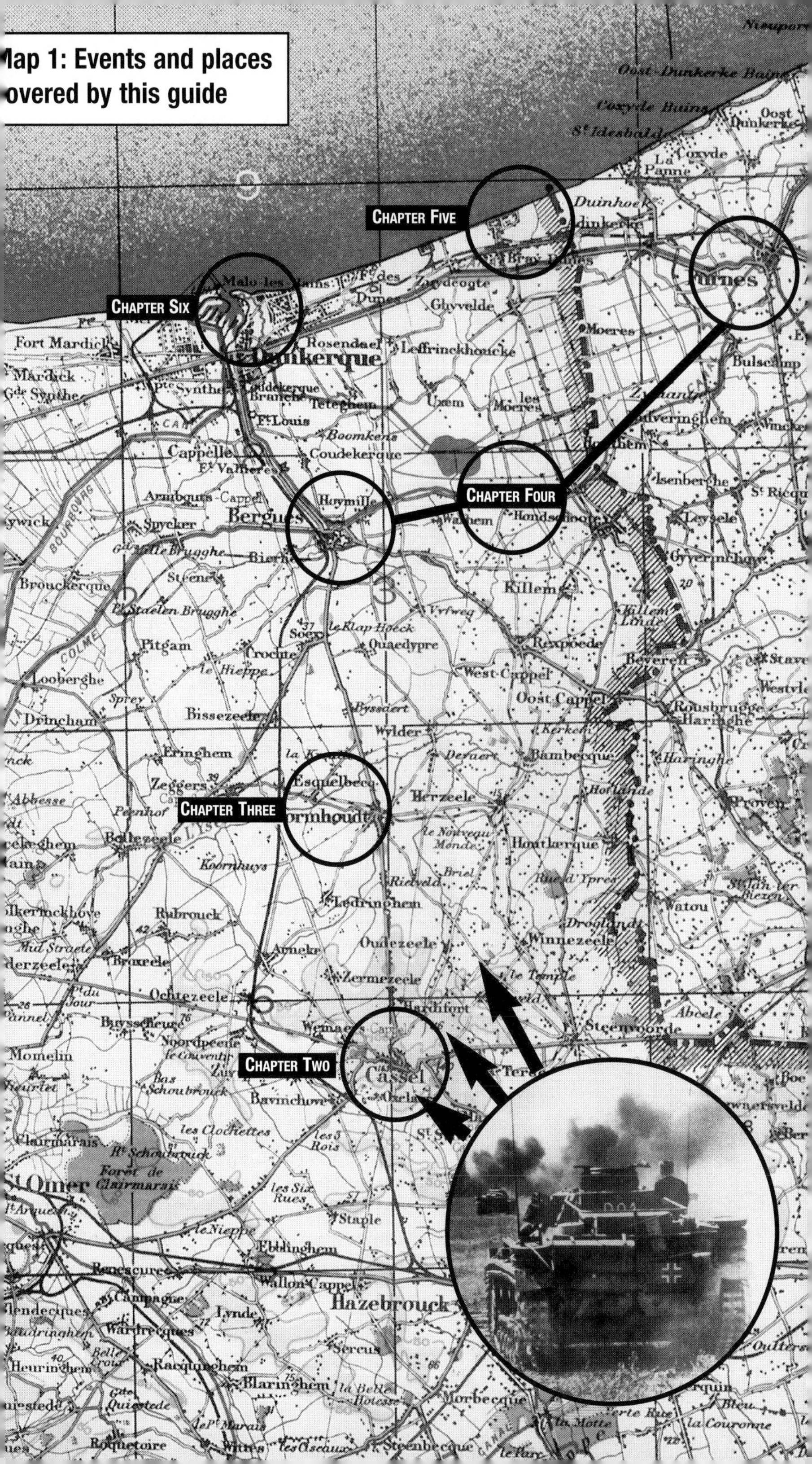

lap 1: Events and places
overed by this guide
Chapter Five
Chapter Six
Chapter Four
Chapter Three
Chapter Two
Malo-les-Bains
Dunkerque
Fort Mardick
Rosendael
Leffrinckhoucke
Ghyvelde
Zuydcoote
Duinhoek
Coxyde
Oost Dunkerke
Furnes
Bulscamp
Moeres
Uxem
Teteghem
Coudekerque
Cappelle
Armbouts-Cappel
Spycker
Bergues
Hoymille
Warhem
Hondschoote
Leysele
Killem
Steene
Broukerque
Pitgam
Socx
Quaedypre
Crochte
Rexpoede
West-Cappel
Oost-Cappel
Beveren
Roesbrugge-Haringhe
Looberghe
Bissezeele
Wylder
Drincham
Eringhem
Zeggers-Cappel
Esquelbecq
Wormhoudt
Herzeele
Bambecque
Houtkerque
Proven
Ledringhem
Rubrouck
Watou
Oudezeele
Winnezeele
Broxeele
Zermezeele
Ochtezeele
Hardifort
Steenvoorde
Abeele
Buysscheure
Noordpeene
Cassel
Momelin
Bavinchove
les Clochettes
Clairmarais
Forêt de Clairmarais
St Omer
Staple
Ebblinghem
Renescure
Wallon Cappel
Hazebrouck
Campagne
Lynde
Wardrecques
Sercus
Racquinghem
Blaringhem
Morbecque
Roquetoire
Steenbecque

ACKNOWLEDGEMENTS

Many veterans and their relatives have been contacted and without their input this book could never have got off the ground. They include Major General V.H.J. Carpenter, President of the Dunkirk Veterans Association, Major General Gordon-Finlayson, Vic Chanter, Shev Seagrave, John Jones, Lawrence Edwards, Edwin Newbould, Ernest Long, Jim Hall, Thomas Jones, Percy McDonald, Ken Naylor, Norman Hammond, Leonard Stribley, Cyril Beard, Mrs A Burrows, Mrs Joan Young, Charles Roundell, Christopher Langley, Jeremy White and Alice Jacklin. I would also like to take this opportunity to mention Rupert Ellis who sadly died during the writing of this book, but whose help I much appreciated.

The Sound Archives at the Imperial War Museum provided many interviews with veterans and I would like to thank Rosemary Tudge and, in particular, Peter Hart for his advice and help throughout. Among those whose recollections have been used are, in alphabetical order, Stanley Allen, Oliver Anderson, Robert Brown, David Cowie, Alfred Cromwell, Harry Dennis, Harold Dibbens, Bert Evans, Brian Fahey, Frank Hurrell, Robert Hill, Stephen Hill, Stephen Hollway, Leonard Howard, James Howe, Peter Jeffreys, Arthur Joscelyne, Thomas King, William Knight, Alfred Leggatt, James Moulton, Charles Nash, Ian Nethercott, Thomas O'Brien, John Paisley, John Pearce, Stanley Priest, Edgar Rabbets, Walter Richardson, Douglas Smith, Alfred Tombs, Robert Tong, Ernest Victor, George Viner, Elliot Viney, Peter Wells, George West and Allan Younger. The work done by the oral historians at the IWM is, in my opinion, vital, enabling history to live on through the recollections of the men who shaped it.

The Glosters' Museum was extremely interesting and had a lot of fascinating, well-preserved accounts of the events during this time. I would thoroughly recommend it to anyone interested in regimental histories. Major C.P.T. Rebbeck at the Glosters, Corporal Bingley at the Coldstream Guards archives, and Alan Kear working with the Grenadiers were particularly helpful in finding out details and photographs about their regiments during the time of the withdrawal. I am also very grateful to Alex Acton for her translation work and Jonathan Hanson for managing to unearth some excellent anecdotes regarding this extraordinary event.

I must say a big thank you to George Chamier for his interest and sound words of wisdom. I much appreciated the generous amounts of time and whisky we shared discussing this project. Indeed I have valued the professional input by other members of the Bradfield College History Department as a whole. Charles Hewitt and the team at Pen and Sword also deserve a special mention for all their efforts and, in particular, Roni Wilkinson's eye for a good photograph, enthusiasm and humour.

Most of all, I am hugely indebted to my father for his constant encouragement and help throughout. His proof reading, map-drawing and his excellent company and advice on our tour around the battlefield sites were invaluable in making this book possible.

'The unbeaten Army moves to a new front', was the original catch line for this photograph taken at Dover as the ships crowded with British troops sail into the harbour. TAYLOR LIBRARY

INTRODUCTION

If any event has come to embody a nation's spirit, then it is surely the 'miracle of Dunkirk'. But the reality of what happened in those midsummer weeks in 1940 has been transmuted into myth, and myths make bad history. I have tried to remind the reader of what really happened.

My aim has been to paint the background to the events on the beaches, as well as to tell the story of the evacuation itself. The speed and ferocity of the German drive through Belgium and France had a devastating effect on the British Expeditionary Force and their French allies, and the fighting retreat to Dunkirk is an intrinsic part of the story. General Gort's decision to set up strongpoints, in order to create an escape corridor, and the desperate rearguard actions that took place on these and along the perimeter defences are vital to an understanding of the climactic events on the beaches and the Mole. In recounting the BEF's remarkable escape, I have tried to balance consideration of the strategic picture with examination of many individual engagements. Each chapter starts with a brief topographical account to set the scene for the visitor to the battlefield, and ends with a list of suggested sites to visit.

No account is, of course, complete without full reference to the role of the Royal Air Force, the Royal Navy and the legendary 'little boats'. I have also dwelt at some length on the qualities of the Commanders, while at the same time letting the ordinary soldier tell his story.

Dunkirk was a disastrous military setback, but it was not a defeat. Thanks to generally superb leadership from the top down, heroism in the face of overwhelming odds, improvisation and 'true grit', a desperate situation was somehow salvaged. To that extent, the myth of Dunkirk is true. Dunkirk gave Britain a second chance, without which the course of the war would have been drastically different. But there are other aspects of the myth which do not bear scrutiny. I hope that I have succeeded in shattering some illusions, while at the same time illuminating the true nature of the miracle that saved the British army.

Chapter One

FROM SITZKRIEG TO BLITZKRIEG

At midnight on 4 June 1940, Hitler decreed that bells should be tolled throughout the Reich for three days. Dunkirk had fallen. The last four weeks had witnessed the most devastating offensive in the history of warfare. The contrast to the gruelling stalemate on the same battlefields in the Great War could not have been more startling. Not even the greatest pessimist could have predicted that the entire British Expeditionary Force would be driven back into the sea in less than a month. The 'miracle' of Dunkirk is that it managed to evacuate at all. The strewn stores and equipment, around the port and nearby beaches, enough for 500,000 men, bore testament to the haste and desperation of the withdrawal. How had this happened?

Declaration of War

On 3 September 1939, Britain reluctantly declared war. At 11.15am that day Neville Chamberlain, the Prime Minister, broke the news to the nation over the BBC. As Germany had failed to respond to the Anglo-French ultimatum to withdraw from Poland, he said in a weary and resigned voice, Britain and Germany were at war. The air raid sirens in London wailed less than half an hour after the announcement. A nation braced itself. It was scarcely believable that another war could follow so soon after the carnage of 1914-18. The fear was that modern technology, as witnessed in the devastating power of the Luftwaffe bombing raid at Guernica during the Spanish Civil War, would lead to unprecedented civilian casualties. A

Mussolini and Hitler with Dr Schmidt and Neville Chamberlain carving up Czechoslovakia on 29 September 1938.

million burial forms had already been printed, and the Imperial Defence Committee estimated that around 600,000 would be killed during the first day of bombing.

It is little wonder therefore that the massive majority of the British public backed Chamberlain's policy of appeasement in the late 1930s. Indeed, he had been welcomed back from Munich in 1938 as a hero. People chose to forget that, in averting war, he had dishonourably accepted Hitler's demand for the Czech Sudetenland. The Czech Government under Benes was not even consulted, but, for Britain, it was 'peace in our time'. Winston Churchill and a few others were lone voices in opposition. He told the Commons:

> *'We have been defeated without a war. And do not suppose that this is the end. This is only the first bitter drink which will be forced on us year by year. Unless we rise again. And take our stand for freedom as in the olden times.'*

For some years, Churchill had viewed events across the channel with alarm. As early as October 1935 he warned:

> *'The whole of Germany is an armed camp. Everyone is being trained from childhood up to war. A mighty army is growing up - great cannon, tanks, machine guns and poison gas. The German Airforce is growing at a great speed'*

A Polish comment on Britain's inactivity. The words read: *'Britain! This is your work!'*

Feet up! A Grenadier Guards foot inspection in France, November 1939

Few people listened. While Hitler tore up the Treaty of Versailles with a massive rearmament programme, with the remilitarization of the Rhineland, with the banned Anschluss with Austria, with the occupation of the Sudetenland and, lastly, the whole of Czechoslovakia, Britain and France did nothing. The invasion of Poland changed everything. At 5.00pm on the same day as the British declaration of war on Germany, the French Government under Daladier with even greater reluctance announced its own belligerence.

Hitler was shaken by the news. It had been totally unexpected, as Albert Speer, later one of his leading ministers, recalled in his memoirs:

> *'Hitler was initially stunned but quickly reassured himself and us by saying that England and France had declared war merely as a sham, in order not to lose face before the whole world. There would be no fighting; he was convinced of that, he said.'*

He was soon proved wrong. Whilst the Allies did nothing effective to protect the nation on whose behalf they had gone to war, their conviction was made all too apparent when the first of 300,000 soldiers of the British Expeditionary Force, led by Lord Gort, made their way across the Channel that month.

Lord Gort VC

Profile of Lord Gort

John Standish Surtees Prendergast Vereker, 6th Viscount Gort, was 54 years old when he led the BEF into France. To many, his appointment came as a surprise. He had never commanded any unit larger than a brigade and his various staff jobs at home and in India after the First World War hardly seemed ideal training for such a post. His reputation for bravery had, however, already reached legendary status by the time he set off to France. During the Great War he was wounded four times and was mentioned in despatches nine times. It is hard to know which is more astonishing, his bravery or his survival. He had also won the Military Cross, the Distinguished Service Order and two Bars and finally the Victoria Cross, when commanding his battalion at the crossing of the Canal du Nord in September 1918 (close to where Guderian crossed it in the opposite direction in May 1940). From the moment he joined the Grenadier Guards in 1905, it was clear he was an outstanding leader of men. There was, however, less certainty about his ability to lead a whole expeditionary force. He was no intellectual, but he possessed commonsense and was adored by his troops, who referred to him by the affectionate, if rather unflattering, nickname 'Fat Boy'. This was despite a concerted effort by Army Public Relations to encourage the press to nickname him 'Tiger'. Lieutenant General Alan Brooke, who was not averse to criticizing his generals, highlighted his abilities:

> *'One of those pre-eminently straight characters who inspired confidence. He could never have done anything small or mean... . He had one of those cheerful dispositions full of vitality, energy and* joie de vivre, *and the most wonderful charm, and was gifted with great powers of leadership... . I could not help admiring him and had feelings of real and deep affection for him.'*

But he also added:

> *'I had no confidence in his leadership when it came to handling a large force. He seemed incapable of seeing the wood for the trees.'*

Critics argued that, on arrival in France, he buried himself under pedantic details at the expense of developing a strategy. His French colleagues were patronizing towards him and showed little confidence in his tactical ability. Certainly his simple tastes were in stark contrast to their liking of Cadillacs, expensive meals and elaborate uniforms. When the German offensive began, Gort was under instructions to take his orders from the French High Command, unless he received an order which appeared 'to imperil the British Field Force'. His interpretation of this command would later save the BEF.

The pressure on Gort during the devastating German offensive of May 1940 cannot be exaggerated. As the situation worsened, he became convinced that only evacuation would save the BEF. With dogged determination and deflected neither by the arguments of the French Generals nor by those of Churchill to move his force south, he formed the strongpoints and Allied escape corridor that were to make the evacuation possible.

The Phoney War

From the outset the Allies prepared for siege warfare of the type experienced in the First World War. Over 1.3 million Frenchmen had lost their lives in the Great War, largely as a result of attacking well-defended German lines. The natural reaction was that the French Generals and Government demanded a policy of *défense à l'outrance*. As a result of this thinking, in the 1920s Andre Maginot, the Minister of War, initiated a line of fortifications designed to prevent any chance of a German invasion on to French soil. A massive 87,000,000 francs was spent making this 'western front in concrete' totally impassable. It probably was, but unfortunately it only provided for a defence of the Franco-German border, which was the Germans' least likely approach. Naïvely, it relied totally on the sanctity of Belgium neutrality. Perhaps the most worrying aspect of the Maginot Line

British troops entering one of the Maginot Line forts in November 1939. Lord Gort made arrangements with the French for British units to serve alongside their allies in a bid to heighten cooperation.
TAYLOR LIBRARY

was psychological. It engendered a sense of false security, of sitting behind an impregnable iron fence.

The competence of the French Generals was also in doubt. Several British Generals found themselves singularly unimpressed with the attitudes and policies of the French High Command. This was cause for serious concern, since, owing to Britain's small professional land army of four divisions (increased to ten by May 1940) compared to France's ninety-four divisions, all strategic decisions had to be left to the French. At a lunch with his Allied generals, Lieutenant General Alan Brooke, commanding II Corps, asked a question about defences to which he received the reply, *'Ah bah! On va les faire plus tard – allons, on va déjeuner!'* Later that night he wrote, 'I could not help wondering whether the French are still a firm enough nation to take their part on seeing this war through'. His pessimism was further confirmed after attending an official showing of a French Army film. *'A very amateur appearance,'* he commented *'which compares unfavourably with the efficiency of the Germans.'*

It is little wonder that the French Army seemed unimpressive, given the climate of strong anti-militarism that had pervaded the country in the 1920s and 30s. The Nazis, by contrast, had been quick to stifle such pacific thought. Books such as Remarque's *All Quiet on the Western Front*, which reminded people of the horror and wastefulness of war, were burned. Since his arrival in power in 1933, Hitler had carefully prepared a nation for war. The young, in particular, were targeted. As early as ten, they joined the *Jungvolk*, pledging *'to devote all my energies and strengths to the saviour of our country, Adolf Hitler. I am willing and ready to give up my life for him so help me God'.* Strong emphasis was placed on physical culture and disciplined teamwork. Military training was an integral part of the Hitler Youth which boys joined at fourteen. By the age of eighteen, when the boys were conscripted, they were thoroughly trained in marksmanship, drilling, leadership skills, parachute jumping and survival.

Like the French Army, the British Forces were also unprepared to face the Nazi war machine. The only adequate tank that the BEF possessed was the 'Matilda' of which there were only sixteen in early 1940. Rearmament had taken off very slowly during the appeasement years. Indeed, the wooden-wheeled artillery of the Great War was still in use during skirmishes with the Italians in the Egyptian-Libyan desert as late as 1938-39. On arrival in France, the BEF found itself desperately short of ammunition, guns and anti-aircraft protection. Furthermore, some of the units arriving from England were completely untrained. Montgomery, having inspected one machine-gun battalion towards the end of November, described it as totally unfit for war in every respect. *'It would be sheer massacre to commit it to action in its present state'*. His memoirs, with the benefit of hindsight, had harsh words for the British Army as a whole,

Von Schirach, leader of the Hitler Youth, accompanies the Führer during an inspection of the youngsters at a rally. Throughout the 30s the German people were being readied for war, whilst at the same time the British and the French viewed militarism with disfavour.

stating that it was:

> *'Totally unfit to fight a first-class war on the continent... .In the years preceding the war, no large-scale exercise for troops had been held in England for some time. Indeed the regular army was unfit to take part in a realistic exercise.'*

Fortunately, the expected offensive never arrived. The bitter winter prevented Hitler from launching an attack on the ill-equipped and unprepared Anglo-French army. The 'phoney war' gave the Allies some much-needed time to prepare. James Langley, a twenty-three-year-old subaltern in 2/Coldstream Guards, found himself endlessly practising retreat and rearguard actions. One day he approached his Company commander about the reasons for this. *'We always start a war with retreat. What makes you think it will be different this time?'* was the reply. Little did Langley know how invaluable such training would be.

The soldiers of the BEF seem to have found the cold winter of 1939 dull. They were away from home and many soon found the reality of active service far from glamorous. Wine at least was cheap and concert parties provided some relief to the boredom. By special permission conducted parties of the British troops were taken to visit the Maginot Line, against

Gracie Fields, the popular Lancashire singer, entertains British soldiers somewhere in France during the Phoney War period.

which the Germans were expected to hurl themselves. A number found the wide selection of brothels a more educational experience. In the first month of the war, Montgomery noted that forty-four cases of venereal disease had been reported to his divisional medical services. His enquiries found that a number of men were subsidizing the local girls for favours 'in the beetroot fields', as well as frequenting unlicensed brothels. He urged his junior commanders to point out to their men that the Military Police knew where the licensed, and therefore relatively disease-free, brothels were and that 'any soldier who is in need of horizontal refreshment would be well advised to ask a policeman for a suitable address'. The order got Monty into much trouble, but his reputation did not suffer amongst his men who jokingly referred to him as the 'General of Love'.

For the most part, though, the BEF laboured building defences along the Franco-Belgian border. The soldiers became sick and tired of constant digging, building and wiring, and it was not long before they referred to this period of calm as the 'Bore War'. Forty miles of anti-tank obstacles, fifty-nine airfields, 400 concrete pillboxes and over 100 miles of broad gauge railways were built that winter. The irony is that when war finally came, these defences were never used. This was because General Gamelin, the French Commander-in-Chief, let political considerations outweigh military ones. His plan stated that, in order to protect Belgium, the Allies should leave their well-prepared positions and move into Belgium to halt the German offensive along the River Dyle.

Gamelin made another fateful miscalculation. He believed the valleys and forests of the Ardennes to be impassable and ignored advice to keep central reserves there in case of attack. Instead, he decided to deploy enormous amounts of troops on his flanks, along the Belgium and Swiss borders. The consequences of this strategy would soon become dramatically clear.

Many Allied leaders were taken by surprise when fighting did finally break out. The War Office had viewed the front as one of stalemate and the Prime Minister, Neville Chamberlain, predicted on 4 April that *'Hitler had missed the bus'*. Five days later German troops invaded Denmark and Norway, and the public realized that Chamberlain's optimism was unfounded. The Norwegian campaign that followed was a disaster for Britain, resulting in the hitherto complacent Parliament turning on the Prime Minister and his administration. Leo Amery MP provided the climax of a hectic Commons debate, exhorting Chamberlain to resign with the

British soldiers became sick and tired of constant digging, building and wiring, and it was not long before they referred to this period of calm as the 'Bore War'.

words:

'You have sat too long here for any good you are doing. Depart, I say, and let us have done with you. In the name of God, go!'

On 10 May 1940, the day the 'phoney war' in France ended, Churchill became Prime Minister.

Blitzkrieg

Nothing had prepared the Allies for the speed of the *Blitzkrieg* attack. On the first day airborne units captured the Belgian fortress of Eben Emael and, within 24 hours, German ground forces had swept across the Dutch border and linked up with them. Other airborne troops landed alongside key river crossings and the route into Belgium soon lay open. Meanwhile, the Stuka divebombers destroyed airfields and cause widespread panic, whilst Panzers exploited the confusion and uncertainty by punching their way deep into enemy territory.

Unaware of the devastating effects the blitzkrieg was having ahead of them, the BEF advanced as planned towards the Dyle line, a few miles east of Brussels, to meet General Bock's Army Group B. When he heard of the Allied advance into the Low Countries, Hitler said afterwards, *'I could have cried for joy – they had fallen into the trap'*.

Blitzkreig in action. A Czech-designed light tank Panzerkampfwagen 38(t), during the drive through France in May 1940.

The reason for his delight soon became clear. Gamelin had miscalculated and the main German thrust was in fact further south. Seven of the ten German divisions forming General von Rundstedt's Army Group A attacked through the Ardennes, which the French believed to be so impenetrable that they had neglected to build the Maginot line on its front. Their success was startling. By 13 May the Germans had reached France. Bridgeheads across the River Meuse were formed, and it seemed that only the French fortress of Sedan could halt their advance.

On 14 May, a massive fleet of Allied bombers attempted to bomb the German bridgeheads and slow the momentum of the offensive. Of the 170 planes (100 of them British), eighty-five were shot down by anti-aircraft guns which the Germans had moved up to form the spearhead of the advance. Air Marshal Barratt, commanding the British Air Force in France, wept at the news. He was

German troops during their surge through Belgium and France in May 1940. The speed and professionalism of the advance left the Allies reeling.

not alone. Emotions were running high throughout the Allied commands as news of setbacks in the Ardennes reached them. Andre Beaufré, a junior staff officer at French General Headquarters, recalled;

> *'The atmosphere was that of a family in which there had been a death. General Georges... was terribly pale. "Our front has been broken at Sedan. There has been a collapse." He flung himself into a chair and burst into tears. It made a terrible impression on me. Doumenc (Georges' subordinate) – taken aback – reacted immediately, "General, this is war and in war setbacks are bound to happen!" Then Georges, still pale, explained: following terrible bombardment from the air the two inferior divisions (55 and 7) had taken to their heels. X Corps signalled that the position was penetrated and that the German tanks were in Bulson (two miles west of the Meuse and so inside the French defended area). Here was another flood of tears. Everyone else remained silent, shattered by what had happened. "Well General," said Doumenc, "all wars have their costs. Let's look at the map and see what can be done".'*

It was too late. By 15 May Sedan had fallen and now nothing stood in the way of the Panzers. There was further shock when, instead of advancing on Paris as the French Commanders had expected, they now turned toward the Channel coast. For Major-General Erwin Rommel, commanding the 7th Panzer Division, the only problem he faced was that he lacked enough maps. The French garages he passed, however had more

Lord Gort and Air Marshal Barratt. Outdated British bombers were being shot out of the skies as they attempted to stall the German attack.

than enough Michelins. He recorded the scene on the roads, as his Panzers rolled on through France unhindered:

> *'Civilians and French troops, their faces distorted with terror, lay huddled in the ditches and in every hollow beside the road... Always the same picture, troops and civilians in wild flight down both sides of the road... A chaos of guns, tanks and military vehicles inextricably tangled with horse-drawn carts... . By keeping our guns silent and occasionally driving alongside the road we managed to get past without great difficulty.'*

Whilst Rommel was making good progress, it was General Heinz Guderian who was stealing the show.

Profile of General Guderian

Above all others, 'Fast Heinz' Guderian was the man who made the blitzkrieg concept such a devastating reality in 1940. He was the chief theoretician and creator of the Panzer divisions. Yet, surprisingly, for much of his career, he had had nothing to do with mechanization. In the Great War, he served as a signals specialist and intelligence officer. It was his experience of offensives such as Verdun, which resulted in the death of 350,000 Germans, that had persuaded him to work out ways of avoiding the unnecessary slaughter of static warfare.

Guderian soon became an expert on the effect of motorization on military mobility and in his lectures in the late 1920s he strongly advocated a primary role for tanks in battle. His book *Achtung-Panzer!*, unfortunately never translated into British or French, argued that tanks were at their most effective if fighting in large units, which provided the maximum concentration of firepower. Their aim must be to not just break into the enemy front but through it, where they could then proceed to knock out reserves and headquarters. Once this had occurred, motorized infantry could 'mop up'. The secret of success was, however, surprise. This posed a problem because he also believed that the enemy should be 'softened' up before the Panzers went in, and prolonged artillery bombardment would give the game away. Stukas soon provided the answer.

These ideas were revolutionary and not always well received by the conservative Wehrmacht generals. One famous exchange with General Bock highlighted the opposition that Guderian was up against:

> *'Tank armour prevents men from saluting properly on parade. Anyway you move too fast. How can you ever command all that without telephones? Bock argued. "By radio," replied Guderian. "Wrong!" retorted the conventional General, "Wireless will never work in a tank".'*

Guderian's ideas did, however, have the support of the man whose opinion really mattered. Hitler strongly believed in this plebeian officer's doctrine. Indeed, on viewing a demonstration of Germany's earliest tank prototype, he exclaimed repeatedly to Guderian, *'That's what I need! That's what I want!'* By October 1935, the first Panzer Divisions were formed, when the young Guderian was still only a Colonel. Under Hitler's patronage Guderian, regarded as pro-Nazi, rose quickly up the military ladder. In 1939, as a full General, his Panzers proved more than their worth during the invasion of Poland.

Seven months later, as part of General Colonel Gerd von Rundstedt's Army Group A, Guderian's XIX Panzer Corps crashed through the Ardennes and, thrusting towards the coast, cut the Allied Northern and Southern armies in two. His leading tanks were positioned only ten miles away from Dunkirk on 24 May when he received the extraordinary 'Halt Order'. In fourteen days Guderian's Panzers had revolutionized warfare and brought the Allied armies to their knees.

Heinz Guderian

Later his Chief-of-Staff, General Nehring, reflected on this spectacular advance through France and on the man who had led it:

'Guderian had good reason to be proud of his tank corps, created by him in the face of such strong opposition. Men and equipment had satisfied all the demands placed on them, and we looked forward to the next phase with confidence. The men held their general in high regards, and everybody knew 'Fast Heinz' because he was always with them in the thick of the battle – often further forward than tactically advisable.'

In September 1940 he was promoted to Colonel General and commanded the 2nd Panzer Division in its advance on Moscow. He never recovered from the subsequent failure of the campaign and developed heart failure soon after. He survived the war and lived on until 1954 when, aged 66, he died of ill health.

The Withdrawal

The whole Allied line was pulled back – first to the River Seine, next to

Guderian ('Fast Heinz') in his command vehicle during the campaign in France.

the River Dendre, then to the Escaut. For many British soldiers it was a bewildering experience as the Expeditionary Force had repulsed the enemy on the forty-mile line that they held. Few knew that Rundstedt's Army Group A was outflanking them.

Where possible Sappers blew up bridges to hinder the German advance. Corporal John Jones, South Wales Borderers, found himself an unexpected member of one of these vital demolition parties. He had been stationed on a farm near Louvain in Belgium. Twenty-four-hour duty in a slit trench there had taken its toll and he must have dozed off. When he awoke his unit had gone. He did not know whether the Germans had passed or not, but realized his only chance lay in walking rapidly in a westerly direction. By chance, on the second day, he met up with a Royal Engineer named Sergeant Parsons, who had lost all his troop either missing or killed. He was, however, determined to carry out the task he had been assigned which was to put a number of bridges out of action. As Parsons had a truck, Jones was left with little option but to join him on this dangerous mission.

> *'The three bridges we had to destroy included one at Geraardsbergen over the River Dendre, then the bridge at Courtrai over the River Leie, and if there was any powder left we would then destroy the bridge over the Ijer at Bergues. At least I now knew where I was heading!'*
>
> *That night we placed eight charges on the bridge. Two were on the uprights and six on the girders. I was anxious to get away I can tell you, but the Sergeant said we must make sure the bridge was destroyed. However, all went well and the two buttresses were blown to bits and the whole bridge fell into the river... .That Burrowite was marvellous stuff.'*

Corporal John Jones

Jones and Parsons went on to complete their mission by blowing up the other three bridges. In doing so, they, and the many other sappers doing similar work, were buying valuable time for the withdrawing Allied forces.

Retreats are always nightmares of confusion and this was no exception. Communication between mobile units became impossible. This was partly because throughout the phoney war the BEF had kept radio silence in the interests of security. The radio network, which was virtually untested, now proved almost useless and messages had to be relayed

The Luftwaffe deliberately targeted columns of refugees. 'This was a massacre. All along the road were people who had been killed, with no arms, no heads, there was cattle lying about dead, there was little tiny children, there was old people - not one or two people but hundreds of them lying about in the road.' TAYLOR LIBRARY

by despatch riders, who all too often found the roads clogged with refugees. Many of these, trundling hopelessly along with their prams and handcarts piled high with all that they now possessed, were old people and children. Mixed up with them were despondent-looking columns of French and Belgian troops with their horse transport. All moved in one direction – to the rear.

Leonard Howard, an NCO in 210 Field Company, Royal Engineers, recalled the difficulties the BEF encountered with the refugees:

> *'Refugees were a damn nuisance, blocking roads with their carts. One can't blame them but from an organization point of view, it was a nightmare. Trying to alleviate the German pressure on us with some offensive action became quite impossible with so many civilians amongst you.'*

To make matters worse, the Luftwaffe deliberately targeted these fleeing civilians. Stukas, in particular, added to the misery of these desperate people in an attempt to hamper the BEF withdrawal. Private Ernie Farrow, 2/Norfolks, witnessed the horrific scenes:

> *'As soon as we started to withdraw again, three of the Stukas came over. Now they took no notice of us, we dived out of the lorries because we expected them to blow us to hell. But they didn't, they simply went over the*

top of us and disappeared in the trees. We heard the machine guns, we heard the sirens, and we heard the bombs dropping. On our left flank we had the Belgian Army and we naturally thought that they'd gone after them. But, after we'd driven down the road three or four miles, we found what they'd done. They'd come over us, left us. But to stop us, they'd machine gunned and bombed these poor refugees. This was a massacre. All along the road were people who had been killed, with no arms, no heads, there was cattle lying about dead, there was little tiny children, there was old people - not one or two people but hundreds of them lying about in the road. This was absolutely a massacre. We couldn't stop to clear the road, because we knew that this is what it was done for – to make us to stop and the Germans would have surrounded us. So we had to drive our lorries over the top of them. This was heartbreaking – really heartbreaking – for us, but we couldn't do anything about it.'

It was not just on the roads that people suffered the wrath of the German Air Force. The bombing of towns was a major feature of the campaign too. One young Territorial Officer with the 92nd Field Division, like so many others, could hardly believe the devastation that such raids left in their wake:

'Just as we arrived on the outskirts of Oudenaarde, a town full of troops and civilians, twenty to thirty German bombers appeared. Minutes later, we found ourselves gazing in amazement. The charming little town had suddenly disappeared and in its place was a cloud of reddish dust and black smoke, pierced here and there by giant leaping flames'.

As often happens to an army in retreat, rumours about what was happening elsewhere spread like wildfire - news that the Panzers were here, there and everywhere; that the French had surrendered; that such and such a battalion had been wiped out, and so on, were commonplace. Some were true but most were fantasy. Rumours that the Germans had placed Nazi infiltrators in advance of their invasion had the most destructive

Refugees fleeing westward pass a British Bren Gun Carrier. Many British soldiers experienced feelings of guilt as they left civilians to face imminent German rule.

A French civilian victim of the Luftwaffe.

effect on the British troops. It is debatable how widespread Fifth Column activity was. What is not debatable is that for many of the retreating troops it became an obsession. Problems arose because, for the average BEF soldier, it was quite impossible to discern the difference between the guttural German and Flemish languages. Suspicions ran high and much time was wasted on fruitless manhunts and arrests. At one point an order was issued that all women encountered should be challenged by rifle, as some troops had reported that some of the enemy were masquerading as members of the opposite sex. Whilst the order was ridiculous, such incidents were witnessed, as Leonard Howard recalls:

'On one occasion we saw two nuns pushing a pram on one of the bridges we had prepared for demolition on the Escaut River. They got to the other side and from their pram pulled out a sub-machine gun. They proceeded to gun down civilians on the bridge, until they themselves were shot.'

Despite the Fifth Column rumours, morale remained extremely high. Under such pressure it would have been easy to crack. Colonel Brian Horrocks felt nothing but pride at the way the British soldiers conducted themselves during the exhausting days and nights of withdrawal:

'Through it all our men marched seemingly indifferent to the chaos around them. I know this will sound most insular, but time after time I thanked my stars that they were British troops in whom disaster brings out

all that is best in our national character. In spite of the desperate situation, there was no chaos. It was a well ordered retreat and, as always when things are really unpleasant, the British sense of humour was much to the fore. When I asked one of my company commanders who had just had a sharp brush with the enemy how he was getting on he replied, "Don't look round, sir, I think we're being followed".'

Yet, no amount of humour could mask the feeling of guilt that many of the BEF felt, as they passed the civilians who now faced imminent German rule.

'If you ask anybody what they remember most clearly about the retreat to Dunkirk they will all mention two things – shame and exhaustion. Shame – as we went back through those white-faced, silent crowds of Belgians, the people who had cheered us and waved to us as we came through their country only four days before, people who had vivid memories of a previous German occupation and whom we were now handing over to yet another. I felt very ashamed. We had driven up so jauntily and now, like whipped dogs, we were scurrying back with our tails between our legs. But the infuriating part was that we hadn't been whipped. It was no fault of ours. All I could do as I passed these groups of miserable people was to mutter, "Don't worry – we will come back". Over and over again I said it.'

Back at Gort's Command Post in Wahagnies, a small French town south of Lille, there was little time to ponder on such emotions. The British Commander-in-Chief's priority was to save the BEF and he now realized it was in serious danger. By 19 May, the Dutch Army had collapsed and many Belgian units had become a rifleless rabble in desperate retreat, leaving a great gap on the BEF's left flank. He was receiving contradictory orders from the French High Command and confusion was reigning. Gort believed that the campaign was as good as lost and began to consider evacuation. Churchill and the War Office were appalled and made it clear that they believed he was overreacting. However, Gort's view was further reinforced by news on 20 May that Guderian's Panzers had reached

Innocents caught up in the lightning German advance.

Abbeville and were wheeling north along the coast, thereby completely cutting off a million or so French, British and Belgian soldiers from the main French Armies in the south.

Arras and the Weygand Plan

General Ironside, the Chief of the Imperial General Staff, flew to Gort's Headquarters with orders for the BEF to march south in order to prevent the German Infantry divisions from linking up with the Panzers. Gort had already decided on a limited offensive but refused to commit the bulk of the BEF to Ironside's plan fearing that his army might find itself encircled. It was decided that Major General Harold Franklyn, with two depleted reserve divisions (amounting to little more than two battalions) and eighty-three tanks, would be sent to secure the defences of Arras. It was hoped that the French would attack northwards in concert with the British operation.

In the end Franklyn's men were forced to go alone, as the French V Corps, under General Réné Altmayer, could not be mustered. Major Vautrin, a special liaison officer, had been sent to urge the General to attack simultaneously but later reported back to the High Command with the news that:

> *'General Altmayer, who seemed tired out and thoroughly disheartened, wept silently on his bed. He told me his troops had buggered off. He was ready to accept all the consequences of this refusal (to go to Arras)... but he could no longer continue to sacrifice the Army Corps of which he had already lost half.'*

Franklyn's mission was ambitious from the start and without the French, it became near impossible. Stukas soon wreaked havoc on his force and his call for Hurricanes came too late. Arras was a failure, but the British troops there had heroically managed to hold their ground for forty-eight hours and give the Germans a nasty scare. The German hesitation that followed over the next week was, to a large extent, due to this action. Von Rundstedt said later:

> *'A critical moment in the drive came just as my forces reached the channel. It was caused by a British counter-stroke at Arras on 21 May. For a short time it was feared that our armoured divisions could be cut off before the infantry divisions could come up and support them.'*

While the fighting at Arras raged, Rundstedt's advanced Panzers, led by Guderian, pushed relentlessly on. One of his divisions took Boulogne, but only after thirty-six hours of hard fighting. By the evening of 24 May he had 200 Panzers within fifteen miles of Dunkirk; two other Panzer divisions were roaring up to join him, and behind them were at least six Wehrmacht Infantry divisions. It seemed that nothing could stop the Panzers from reaching Dunkirk and thwarting the Allies' only chance of

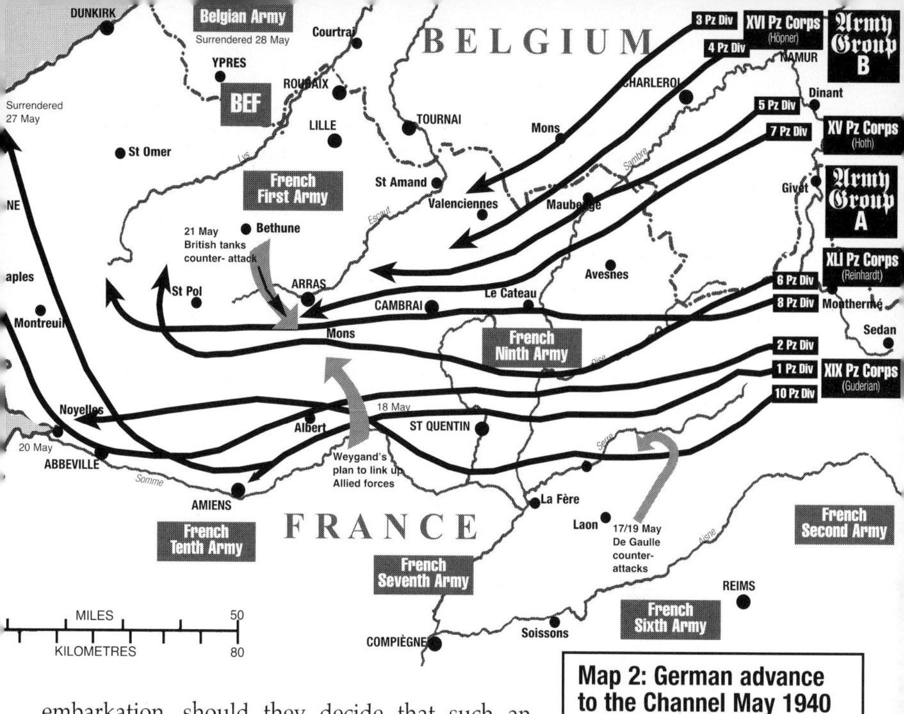

Map 2: German advance to the Channel May 1940

embarkation, should they decide that such an action was necessary. An entry in the First Division's war diary observed, *'It's easier to take prisoners and booty than to get rid of them'*.

Meanwhile General Maxime Weygand had replaced Gamelin and now planned a very large Allied counter-offensive which, like Arras, would link up with the French armies in the south. The BEF was expected to spearhead it with eight divisions and the aid of the French First Army and Belgian Cavalry. Unfortunately and crucially, Gort was not present at the Ypres meeting when the new Commander General had spelled out his plan. Worse still, General Billotte, who was the only man with first-hand knowledge of Weygand's conception, was killed in a traffic accident. His car had skidded into the back of a refugee lorry and, though the driver survived, Billotte was gravely injured and spent two days in a coma before dying. Blanchard, his successor, lacked both the drive and skill needed to organize troops from three different countries into an effective force in less than a few hours. With all co-ordination gone, the Weygand plan was doomed, yet London continued to urge

General Billotte

Gort to cooperate with the French.

In desperation, the BEF Commander urged John Dill, the Vice-Chief of the Imperial General Staff, to come over and see for himself. He got his wish and Dill, after only an hour in France, brought a little relief to the men in London, particularly Churchill, who were still urging action, with the message that, *'There is no blinking the seriousness of the situation in the Northern area'.*

This was no exaggeration. The Belgium line, on the north-eastern side of the BEF's position, was cracking under the pressure of Bock's Army Group B. If it gave way, his troops would have little trouble linking up with Rundstedt's Panzers in the west, thereby completely cutting off the British forces from the coast. Gort's concern was now for the BEF alone. On Saturday 25 May, without asking advice from London and without consulting the French, he made the decision that saved the BEF. He filled the gap between the British left flank and the fast-disintegrating Belgian army with the divisions earmarked for the Weygand plan. This strengthened the Allied pocket, but now left him with only one course of action.

Decision to evacuate

Gort knew that only evacuation would save the BEF and at last, on 26 May, he received the news from Anthony Eden, Secretary of State for War, that he was to proceed:

> *'The only course open to you may be to fight back to the west, where the beaches and port, east of Gravelines will be used for embarkation. Navy will provide fleet of ships and small boats, the RAF will give full support.'*

Even before this telegram, Churchill and Eden had decided that Calais, twenty-four miles west of Dunkirk, must be held to the last man in order to slow down the Panzer advance and buy time for the BEF. For Eden it was a particularly hard decision because among the 3,000 highly trained troops that he was deliberately sacrificing, were the men of the King's Royal Rifle Corps, his old regiment. Eden's order to Brigadier Claude Nicholson, Commander of the Calais garrison, highlighted the importance of their action.

> *'Every hour you continue to exist is of the greatest help to the BEF. The government has therefore decided you must continue to fight. Have greatest admiration for your splendid stand.'*

The garrison fought on for three days, but the truth is that Calais was a strategic decision which had little tactical effect. Guderian only used one division at Calais, the 10th Panzers, which were in fact trailing behind the bulk of his force. He never considered Calais important and his advanced Panzers merely bypassed it.

It was not Calais that bought time for the BEF but an extraordinary

Abandoned French tanks north of La Bassée are passed by motorcycle combinations belonging to 5th Panzer Division.

decision made by their counterparts. With Guderian's Panzers only ten miles from Dunkirk on 24 May, an order came through for them to halt. Hitler had, for over a week, become increasingly worried about the huge inroads the Panzers had made into Northern France. As early as 17 May, General Halder, the Chief of Staff at Army Headquarters, had noted:

'Führer is terribly nervous. Frightened by his own success, he is afraid to take any chances and so would rather pull the reins on us.'

Certain sections of the German High Command had become as apprehensive as their leader about Guderian's advance. The Panzers, they argued, were too far ahead of support fuel, had no chance of maintenance and were down to fifty per cent of their strength. Arras had also served to exasperate their fears. Yet it was Göring, Commander-in-Chief of the Luftwaffe, not the Generals who played the key part in the famous halt order. For the past few days he had been watching with concern the Panzers strangling the Allied armies. Fearful that the tanks were robbing his airforce of glory, he bellowed to his aides, *'This is a wonderful opportunity for the Luftwaffe! I must speak to the Führer at once. Get me a line.'*

Cleverly, he played on Hitler's fears, whilst extolling the virtues of a victory won by a national socialist creation, the Luftwaffe. At 12.41 on the 24th the Führer issued the *'Halt Befehl!'* Guderian was outraged:

'We were utterly speechless, but as we were not told of the reasons for this order it was difficult to argue against it.'

General Walter Nehring, Guderian's Chief-of-Staff, was with his commander at the time of the halt order.

'No reason was given, and Guderian and I assumed the capitulation of

the Allies was imminent. However, as time passed we became very uneasy at the number of ships moving towards Dunkirk – out of artillery range. We reported this, but nothing happened. For two valuable days our opponents were allowed to strengthen their defences.'

The order was lifted on 26 May and preparations were now made for the Panzers to continue the advance. It took sixteen hours before they were ready, as crews needed to be alerted, tanks topped up with fuel and loaded with ammunition, by which time it was dawn on 27 May. The Wehrmacht had lost three full days and, more importantly, the Panzer advance had lost its momentum. Guderian had thought that when the halt order arrived his Panzer divisions could stand down as his message to his men that day reflects:

'I asked you to do without sleep for forty-eight hours, and you endured for seventeen days. I forced you to take... on your flanks and to our rear and you never hesitated. With exemplary confidence and the faith your task could be accomplished you carried out every order in a spirit of self-sacrifice. Germany is proud of her armoured divisions and I consider myself fortunate to have led you. Let us consider with reverence our fallen comrades.'

The halt order and Guderian's subsequent belief that his job was complete might have provided Gort with some encouragement. However, he had so many problems to deal with that, at the time, he could attach little importance to this unexpected windfall. Bologne had fallen, Calais was cut off, the Belgians were crumbling, and, most important of all for the evacuation, the majority of his troops were still deep in France. He made no attempt to conceal the difficult predicament his army faced when, in a reply to Eden's order to evacuate, he stated:

'I must not conceal from you that a great part of the BEF and its equipment will inevitably be lost in the best circumstance.'

Ironside, Chief of the Imperial General Staff, shared Gort's pessimism when later that evening he wrote in his diary:

'Very little chance of the BEF getting off... We shall have lost practically all our trained soldiers by the next few days – unless a miracle appears to help us.'

By coincidence on the day that 'Operation Dynamo' started, a National Day of Prayer for the army in France was already being held. Unknown to the ordinary people there was now something more definite to pray for – the deliverance of the BEF.

'This is a wonderful opportunity for the Luftwaffe! I must speak to the Führer at once.' Göring jumped on the victory bandwagon by assuring Hitler that his Luftwaffe could be trusted to take care of the BEF.

Men of the BEF move to take up new positions as civilian refugees flee from the advancing enemy.

Chapter Two

DEFENCE OF THE STRONGPOINTS

The Panzers' halt provided the Allied Northern Armies with a brief moment to decide on a defensive strategy, in order to get as many soldiers embarked as possible. The French 68th Division moved into the Gravelines area and Gort set up a system of 'stops' and 'strongpoints', which were intended to buy time for the troops flooding back to Dunkirk by providing a necessary escape corridor for them to move down.

All too often the miracle of Dunkirk has been solely linked to the little ships that transported the battle-weary soldiers back to England and, yet without the tremendous fighting spirit of the men defending these strongpoints, the massive evacuation could never have happened.

CASSEL

The D916 runs direct to Cassel from Dunkirk. The town is well signposted and the 178-metre-high hill on which it rests makes it recognizable for miles around. It is not hard to see why General Gort believed that Cassel was such a key strongpoint. It provides the junction for five roads and its large hill, which is in stark contrast to the flat Flanders landscape around it, affords superb views of the surrounding countryside. Its importance as a vital strategic point was recognized long before 1940. Indeed, it was this very hill that became central to the Grand Old Duke of York's ill-fated campaign of 1793-1795, and which became immortalized in the nursery rhyme. In the First World War Marshal Foch and later the popular General Plumer used Cassel as their headquarters, as did General Gort before the withdrawal of the BEF properly.

It is an interesting, relaxed town with cobbled streets, narrow passageways, old buildings and with plenty to do and see. Inevitably the damage inflicted on it during the defiant defence of the town by an assortment of British soldiers, made up mostly of men from the 4th Battalion, The Oxfordshire and Buckinghamshire Light Infantry and 2nd Battalion, The Gloucestershire Regiment, has led to many subsequent

A view of Cassel from the North. The town was a vital strategic point on the flat Flanders landscape.

View across the rooftops of Cassel from Mont Cassel, looking south. It was from this spot that the French commander Maréchal Foch observed the fighting during the Great War of 1914-18.

changes. Nevertheless, the town has successfully managed to retain much of its old charm and is well worth visiting.

Preparation

News that the 2/Glosters were to make their way to Cassel came as a surprise to the Battalion, which had only a few hours before been told it could 'rest' at Nomaine, some miles south-east of Lille, after the rigours and exertions of the past two weeks. They were now told that these would be part of a force made up of 4/Oxf and Bucks, some machine gunners from a territorial Battalion of Cheshires and a few French army anti-tank and machine-gun units under Brigadier Somerset. Their mission was simple – to hold the town 'at all costs'.

The night of 24 May was an eventful one for the exhausted troops who had to contend with a mass of refugees as well as withdrawing British and French soldiers. On reaching Cassel in the early morning, it was clear that the town had already received some attention from the enemy, in the form of a certain amount of bombing from the air. Lance Corporal Young of the Oxf and Bucks, who had arrived just before the Glosters, recalled his first impressions of Cassel:

> *'The streets were cobbled and for the most part narrow. There were some old houses but many had already been destroyed. The main square looked desolate because of the bombing and glass was strewn everywhere. High up stood an old church – looking square, solid and defiant.'*

As the Glosters made their way to the centre of the town, the men noticed an unpleasant smell, which they soon discovered was caused by a number of dead French soldiers and animals. Lieutenant Fane remembers this ominous welcome:

> *'A French artillery unit must have been here previously as the ground was littered with dead mules. We had the unpleasant task of cleaning up the mess.'*

At the time the military situation in the region was extremely vague and reports that some isolated German tanks had broken through and were in the vicinity remained unsubstantiated. The one thing that was certain was that an enemy offensive would occur in the near future and 'Somerforce' had little time to lose if it was to turn the place into a bombardment and tank-proof fortress. Houses and buildings forming a perimeter of the hill were linked by demolition or digging, and strengthened. The men also busied themselves sandbagging, boarding-up windows, caging, making

Map 3: Escape corridor of the British Expeditionary Force showing defensive 'stops' or strongpoints

The Grande Place, Cassel – then and now.

holes in walls for communication and slits for firing. Roads and lanes were blocked, and the few French anti-tank and machine-gun units were utilized to assist in the defence. Unfortunately, initial excitement about the ten French anti-tank guns in the area was short-lived as Captain Lovett explains:

'Soon after, a report was received that these guns were now unmanned and I was sent out to verify the truth of this – it was true, unfortunately, but not only had the men disappeared but they had taken the firing pins with them to render the guns useless'

The local inhabitants provided 'Somerforce' with a further problem. Many refused to leave their homes, hung around public air raid shelters and raised vocal, and sometimes active, objection to the conversion of their houses into defences. This was understandable, but Lieutenant Fane and the other troops preparing the defences of the town had little option but to take firm action:

'When we first arrived, things were very awkward as the civilians had not all cleared out of the town, and we had to turn people out of their houses so that we could fortify them. There were also innumerable spies and Fifth Columnists about and the enemy must have known our position exactly. We were told to particularly beware of stray priests as the Nazis were dropping them in that disguise.'

Eventually Brigadier Somerset ordered all inhabitants to leave under pain of penalties if they refused. That evening nearly all the civilian population were evacuated in buses. Only those too sick or old remained behind with

Diagram of 2/ Glosters' positions at Cassel as recalled by Captain E Jones whilst in captivity.

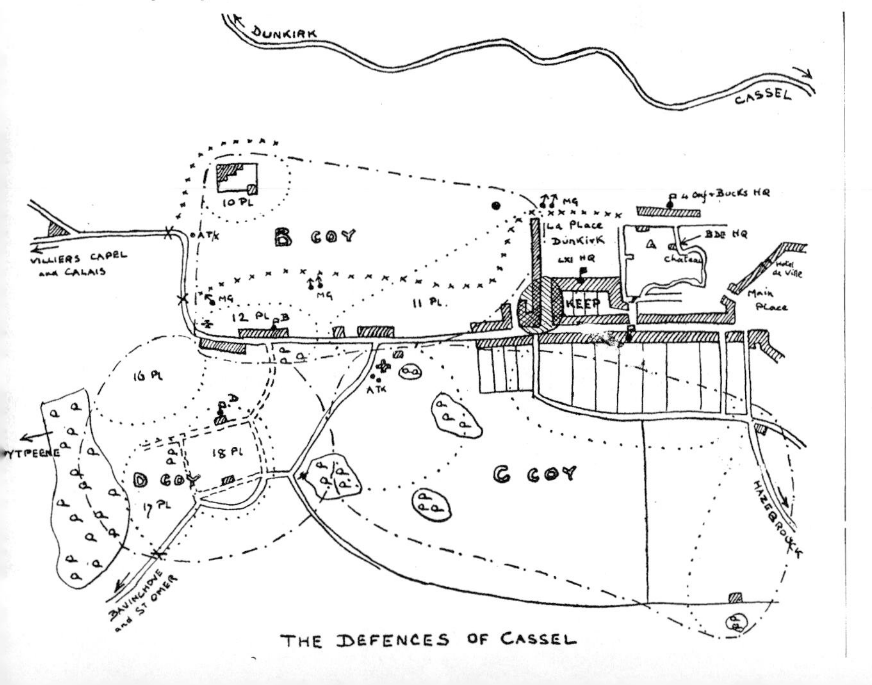

The Sisters of Mercy.

As a result of reconnaissance and co-ordination between the 4/Oxf and Bucks and the 2/Glosters, a circular defence of the town was mapped out, with the Glosters taking up defences in the western half of the town (see map). B Company, linked on its right with the Oxf and Bucks, stretched along the perimeter to the north-west to join D Company, which faced West. Around to the south-west and south and completing the Battalion perimeter was C Company, holding a somewhat more difficult area owing to the minimal field of fire caused by small walled enclosures on the outskirts of the town. The Commanding Officer, Major Gilmore, kept A Company in reserve.

The Glosters took over the local bank and bank manager's house, adjoining, in the Place Dunkirk, and turned it into the Battalion Headquarters. The Oxf and Bucks established their HQ at the Gendarmerie, an ideal place owing to the fact that the prisons and cellars provided more protection than most buildings from the effects of bombardment.

Both regiments were already depleted from the past two weeks' fighting, but the Glosters especially had suffered when on 19 May nine Luftwaffe bombers took advantage of the traffic congestion on the outskirts of Tournai. 194 men of the Battalion were killed or missing as a result of the raid. The Regiment was therefore already thin on the ground and several necessary technical rearrangements had exacerbated this and

Waiting for the enemy. Men of the Gloucestershire Regiment in a hastily built defensive position on the outskirts of Cassel.

left them with virtually no reserves at all.

The first of these was the sending out of A Company's No 1 Platoon under Lieutenant Cresswell to occupy a blockhouse $2^1/_2$ miles north of Cassel, on the road to Dunkirk. The second was the order for the rest of A Company, under Major Percy Hardman, to occupy the village of Zuytpene, west of the town. Similarly D Company of the 4/Oxf and Bucks was sent out to occupy Bavinchove, 2 miles south-east of Zuytpene. These three positions were ordered to break up any enemy assault before it reached Cassel. The men knew their task was an important one but few envisaged the epic struggle they would face over the coming days.

The First Assault – 27 May

On the night of 25 May the troops were able to get a much-needed and uninterrupted sleep. 26 May was also a quiet day but after another night of good rest and preparation, events took a more dramatic and serious turn. After heavy and continuous mortaring and bombing from the air, the

German troops cautiously advancing behind the cover of a tank.

enemy began an all-out offensive on the town. Their main tank and infantry assaults were directed against the south and south-east sides. The Glosters' C and D Companies, and 4/Oxf and Bucks bore the brunt.

Four tanks entered the field below C Company sector and, while one was put out of action, another tank actually managed to enter the small park surrounding Company HQ and inflicted a considerable number of casualties. It was clear that it would have to be dislodged and Captain Wilson, commanding B Company, with the aid of three others and an anti-tank gun, endeavoured to do just that, by outflanking it. One of the men with him was Lieutenant Fane:

'We crept up to within fifty yards of its position and got ready to fire the rifle. Unfortunately, our mortar platoon must have been told to deal with

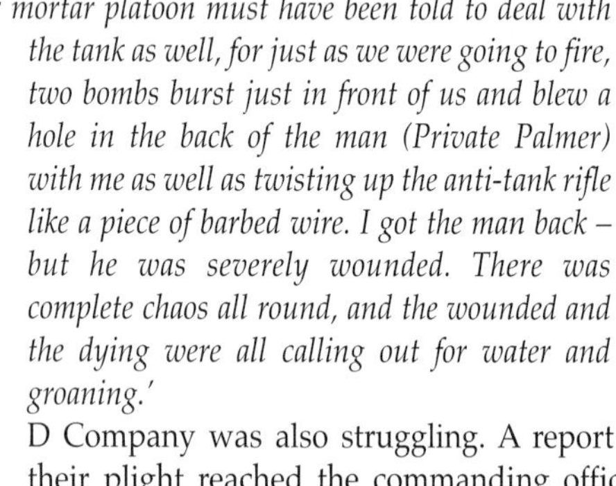

the tank as well, for just as we were going to fire, two bombs burst just in front of us and blew a hole in the back of the man (Private Palmer) with me as well as twisting up the anti-tank rifle like a piece of barbed wire. I got the man back – but he was severely wounded. There was complete chaos all round, and the wounded and the dying were all calling out for water and groaning.'

D Company was also struggling. A report of their plight reached the commanding officer, Major Gilmore, but he was unable to offer Captain Cholmondely any reinforcements as all his company were engaged. Major Gilmore takes up the story:

'D Company reported that enemy infantry

Major Gilmore

were attempting to establish themselves in some cottages just south of their position. I ordered the company to dislodge them with the bayonet. Cholmondely, taking a party of six men, managed to work up to their cottages, which had been originally occupied by machine gunners the previous day, but who had either been put out of action or had evacuated their position without informing anyone. The party got into the cottages, killed one man while the others cleared off.'

This heroic action eased the pressure on D Company which by this stage was down to just forty-eight men (from approximately 120). Elsewhere, Cassel's defences held. The 4/Oxf and Bucks were in the thick of the action and gallantly staved off wave after wave of German assaults.

'A' Company at Zuytpene

Sadly, it is not quite true to say that all the defences held because the company of Oxf and Bucks at Bavinchove were overrun earlier that day. Brigadier Somerset, on hearing the news that it was in enemy hands, sent an order for Major Percy Hardman's A Company at Zuytpene to be withdrawn, realizing that a stand against such superior numbers of on-coming enemy would be futile. The order never got through, despite repeated attempts. With the line cut, despatch riders persistently attempted to get past the Germans. In a last desperate effort, an armoured carrier was sent in with a mission to break through to them. Later that day a burnt-out vehicle with two charred bodies inside was found just outside the defences.

The men of A Company at Zuytpene were themselves also desperately attempting to make contact with the rest of the Battalion at Cassel. Every attempt was thwarted – a despatch rider was shot in the chest soon after leaving their position and a further two runners also failed to get through. They had faced continuous bombardment since early morning when nine enemy dive-bombers devastated the town. By 11.00am the enemy was causing much anxiety through heavy and very accurate use of mortars, guns and machine guns on their position (west of the town). Major Percy Hardman recalls the situation by mid-afternoon

Major Percy Hardman

'The Company was suffering heavy casualties; some of the wounded walked and others were carried to Company Headquarters, but many sadly had to lie where they were wounded. The Company Headquarters was frequently hit by shellfire but the cellar, though filled with smoke, was tenable. (It included twenty

All attempts by despatch riders to reach Zuytpene were thwarted. Cassel was surrounded.

> *wounded, two old women and a drunken French soldier). Lance Corporal Harrington twice came back to report that he was the only man left in his section. On the first he was given two men from other sections, on the second occasion, two from Headquarters, whom he cheerfully led back to his post. PSM Oxtoby's platoon was almost non-existent and able to resist no longer.'*

By 18.00 hours the few remaining survivors made their way to the Company HQ. The house was then barricaded. By now there was little chance of any effective defence. Their position was completely surrounded, they had only one Bren gun in action and ammunition, in spite of collecting that of wounded men, was nearly exhausted. Nevertheless, a German assault by seventy infantry was still resisted until the attackers reached the house itself and began throwing grenades into the cellar. At this point Percy-Hardman realized that further resistance was of no value and surrendered.

Amazingly two men from A Company, Privates Tickner and Bennett, who had been sent by Percy Hardman just prior to the final German assault, did somehow reach the rest of the Battalion later that night.

The Blockhouse

At the same time that the defence of Zuytpene was drawing to a close, the platoon at the lone blockhouse north of Cassel faced a furious attack. For the next two days the platoon repeatedly held off enemy assaults. By the 29 May their frustrated opponents began using any tactics they could to knock out the blockhouse. On one occasion they made a wounded British Artillery Captain, whom they had captured previously, move up to the blockhouse and shout, *'A wounded British officer here'*. Lieutenant Cresswell, commanding the men in the blockhouse, answered him but the

Captain whispered back, *'Do not reply'*. When he got to the east side of the building he looked down at a dead German lying there and said out loud, *'There are many English and Germans like that round here.'* As he spoke these words, he looked up at the roof of the blockhouse. This action alerted Cresswell and his men that some Germans had approached from the blockhouse's blind spot and climbed onto the scaffolding in the rear. Part of the building was set on fire but, wearing gas masks, the platoon controlled the stream of smoke drifting down by using a damp blanket, which they kept wet with foul water from the well inside the building.

By 30 May the platoon had completely exasperated the Germans with their defiant defence of their position. It was only later that evening when the enemy brought in heavier weapons and had their troops on the roof again that Cresswell believed further resistance was useless. His orders had been to delay the enemy's approach 'at all costs' and he and his men had done just that for four days under terrible conditions. With no rations, no medical assistance for the wounded and with the building on fire for 36 hours, their efforts seem all the more remarkable. Lieutenant Cresswell was later awarded the MC (as was Percy Hardman for his heroics at Zuytpene). However, he was quick to pay tribute to the men of his platoon:

> *'Throughout the whole of our sojourn in the blockhouse, their morale, grit, fortitude and perseverance were excellent. Despite the order of "One hour on, one hour off", resulting in little sleep and the lack of food and water, they remained cheerful throughout and fought well right up to the fall of the blockhouse.'*

Lieutenant Cresswell MC

The Blockhouse north of Cassel on the D916 overlooking the crossroads at Peckel. Signs of the fighting can still be seen in the scarred concrete. You will need permission from the farmer to visit this interesting site.

Courtesy of Nicolas Marliot/Julien Depret

Men of 144 Brigade captured on the outskirts of Cassel.

Cassel – 28/30 May

Back at Cassel, the rest of 'Somerforce' were showing the same spirited defence as their comrades outside the town. After the heavy German assault on the 27 May, the fighting died down for a day. Sniping was rife and the enemy artillery continued to bombard their positions, helped no doubt by Fifth Columnist activities in the town. Brigade and Battalion headquarters were particularly affected, and the former was forced to move into the Gendarmerie where the Oxf and Bucks were based. Yet even here there was no hiding from the effects of the German artillery, as Lance Corporal Young remembers:

> *'I was on the ground floor with a member of the Orderly Room Staff during the uproar, and we had decided that one place was as safe as any other when two shells burst in quick succession, one just to the left of us, and the other just to the right. It was then that I suggested that the next one might get us and so we made for the cellar. I had just arrived at the foot of the cellar stairs when there was a crash. The crowded cellars were full of fumes and brick dust and there was, for a while, confusion, darkness, spluttering and coughing. With the aid of a re-lighted candle, I saw a hole some four or five feet wide, had been made in the ground. The shell had exploded at ground level and the ceiling above had fallen in. Buried under this debris was the ashen face of a Major – there was no doubt about his being dead. If the shell had exploded in the cellar one wonders how many*

survivors there would have been.'

During the day's bombardment the troops continued to strengthen their defences. Cassel had by now been in flames for two days and its defenders, whilst weary, maintained a high morale despite German attempts to discourage them with leaflet drops. Lance Corporal Young commented:

'The leaflets asked us to surrender and informed us that we were surrounded. Nobody showed any signs of believing them, although everyone knew it was true or almost true.'

One of the reasons why the troops privately suspected they were surrounded was that they had received no rations or supplies of any kind since their arrival in the town. As a result the troops were forced to rely on from resources to make up for their half-rations, as Young recalls:

'Looting was, of course, forbidden but there can be no doubt that most men did it. At first smashing into places to get food didn't seem a very pleasant thing to do but as the town, from day to day, crumpled under shell fire it seemed and became less of a crime.'

Sometimes troops were pleasantly surprised by the delicacies left in these houses and, having lived off their rations for some time, the change of diet that local hoards provided was welcome. Captain Lovett had one such meal spoiled by shellfire:

'We (Brigade HQ) were just thinking of having some lunch – it was going to be a rather good one as I know champagne and chicken had been procured – when crash, a shell landed on our cottage Mess. Only the four batmen were in at the time – none of them were killed but all of them were wounded and, of course, our lunch was spoiled'.

Continuous enemy bombardment took its toll on the British defenders. A number would never leave Cassel.

A leaflet dropped by the Luftwaffe on British positions, spelling out the hopeless situation facing the BEF.

Food soon became the last of the men's worries.

The next day saw the most violent of all the enemy assaults, as they were attacked from three directions simultaneously. It was launched at 9.00am and continued until mid-afternoon. The heavy bombardment preceding and during the battle began to claim a large number of casualties. Eventually the attack petered out, but, as the personal diary of Captain Wilson commanding B Company of the Glosters reveals, it came perilously close to breaching the perimeter he was holding:

> *'Just after breakfast a number of 10 Platoon arrived at my HQ breathless, distressed and with the news that Lieutenant Weightman was killed. The farm they had been in was shelled and mortared so as to become untenable and they had withdrawn. It appeared that Corporal Waite and one of two others had remained. The German infantry had approached to within thirty yards of the farm but had been driven off, and mortaring began again. The stretcher bearers, intensely plucky, went down to do what they could for the wounded, without hesitation, even though the mortaring was now very heavy and the garrison of the farm only three or four.'*

Wilson managed to rally and reorganize the men, and they were ordered to return to a position near the farm. Here they succeeded in holding back the enemy, but it had been a close-run thing.

During the late afternoon a military police despatch rider arrived at Cassel. Although the town was completely surrounded, he had somehow managed to reach it undetected. His message, intended for the previous day, ordered 'Somerforce' to move back to Dunkirk. Lieutenant Fane, like the whole garrison, was stunned:

> *'We had been ordered to hold Cassel to the last round and last man, to cover the withdrawal to Dunkirk, so we did not expect the order to withdraw. By this time the Germans were all round us and we were prepared to settle down to a good fight. Imagine our surprise when we received the message to break for it!'*

All attempts to re-establish radio contact with the troops in Cassel failed. Isolated, under-strength and poorly equipped the men of the Glosters and Oxf and Bucks fought on.

The Breakout

Plans were made to get out after dark. The Battalions were ordered to move with only what each man stood up in – his weapons, equipment and such rations as he could carry. Vehicles were smashed by pickaxe, as burning them might have given the game away. The wounded were collected and placed in a nearby house with some food and water, and a stretcher-bearer who volunteered to remain with them. Here they were left to the mercies of the Germans. Zero hour was 21.30. It was a pitch-black night and only the flames from bombed houses provided any relief from the darkness. In single file the soldiers slowly and quietly began to leave the town.

The 400 remaining men of the 4/Oxf and Bucks were the first to move out. To their surprise they encountered no enemy as they made their way down from Cassel. The pace was brisk as they trekked over fields and through woods, over ditches and through hedges. The odd sound of cows and dogs nearby seemed to disturb the whole countryside. Tension was running high as they pushed silently on. Every man was acutely aware that his freedom and life was at stake around every corner. They were also aware that the region was littered with minefields. For some three hours they made good progress when suddenly their march was halted by small arms fire. Tracer bullets flew past the crouching men from a point some hundred yards away. However, the Battalion was in no state to confront the enemy and, after some time assessing their situation, made a successful detour.

Soon after, at around 3.30am as the early signs of dawn were appearing, the advance party once again came across enemy fire causing the Battalion

The Northern Gate. Along the wall on the right of the picture is a poppy wreath and below it is a plaque commemorating those Glosters who died in the fighting in May.

to change direction. Clearly the hunt was now on and the situation worsened when the column was fired at from the right and the front, while mortar shells began to rain down from the left. The troops, now lining a sunken road track, were soon returning fire with similar ferocity. The noise was terrific and the air was filled with lead as the Battalion fought for its survival. Lance Corporal Young recalls the closing moments of the battle:

> *'Things had not improved after thirty minutes of intense fighting and our casualties were mounting alarmingly. The Adjutant was severely wounded but he remained calm. A stretcher-bearer was called for but, with all the confusion and noise, it was a hard task to locate a bearer. My most vivid memories of this time were the hysterical French citizens who were witnessing the scene, as well as the moans of our wounded. The tide of the battle turned when, suddenly, some six enemy tanks wheeled round into position. They were about 500 yards away and moving towards us. Surprisingly, and to our relief, their guns remained silent. The leading tank commander, a brave man surely, stood up in the turret and shouted for us to surrender. Shame or no shame the Colonel ordered us to pack it in. In the silence that followed we were conscious of a deep depression. We had all known that we might be wounded or killed but few seem to have contemplated the possibility of being taken prisoner.'*

Meanwhile the Glosters had left Cassel and, with Major Gilmore, compass in hand, leading, the party began to make their way toward Dunkirk. The

Battalion was severely depleted, having lost A Company altogether. Progress for the remaining 270 men was slow. There were many halts, and roads were avoided as they were deemed too unsafe. By around 4.00am their attempted escape became unstuck when they encountered considerable enemy resistance. After an unsuccessful battalion assault, they withdrew to a large wood, Bois Saint-Acaire. Their only hope was to take cover during the day and break out at night. Companies were soon ordered to act independently. Unfortunately the Glosters had been spotted entering the wood and heavy mortaring and machine-gun fire pinned down the Commanding Officer and the Battalion Headquarters, who were in a trench system just outside the wood. Gilmore's party had little option but to surrender:

'By 11.30am a heavy machine gun and small shellfire opened up on our trench. Within minutes enemy infantry with fixed bayonets appeared on the parapet and as resistance was useless, the Battalion's Headquarters climbed out of their refuge to find themselves surrounded not only by enemy infantry but also four tanks some hundred yards away.'

Meanwhile the companies in the wood itself were also coming under increasingly heavy machine-gun fire. Lieutenant Fane with D Company recalls:

'We must have been spotted by the Hun for we had not been there long before the whole area around the wood resounded with the cries of

Prisoners of War in Stalag VII. Lance Corporal Young is on the far right smoking a pipe.

Captured Tommies are led away by an SS unit. For them the war was over.

"Kamerad! Kamerad!" There were quite a lot of troops shouting this treacherous word at the top of their voices. Then they all stopped and a voice started yelling in very good English, "Come out! Come out! Hitler is winning the war, you are beaten. Come out or we will shell you out. Lay down your arms." It was a nasty moment for us, for we all realized the hopeless position we were in – one false move and we would all be shelled to hell. However, I remembered hearing the story of another battalion which had been ruthlessly machine-gunned on giving itself up. I told this story to the men and we decided to stay where we were and fight to the last. As the Germans knew our position the first thing we had to do was choose another. There was a wood about 100 yards away on the left and we decided to make for that, so, bunching on the edge of the wood we were in, the men waited for the signal to run across the open ground. When it came we all ran like hares. Hardly had we left the wood when machine-gun bullets started whistling all round us. Never before have I run so hard. People were dropping around me but I managed to get across the area and plunge into a thick bush intact.'

Fane and the remaining men of the two companies soon realized they were no better off as further shells rained down on their new positions:

> *'We stayed there all day, and trying to make the time pass was terrible. There was no smoking, no talking above a whisper and as little movement as possible. As we had had no food for a very long time the order was given allowing us to eat our iron rations. Things looked absolutely hopeless, for what chance had two companies against a superior force of Germans backed by tanks and 4" mortars as well as machine guns?'*

When darkness fell, the men moved off but after about an hour they walked straight into an ambush. The devastating effects of machine-gun fire and grenades soon caused heavy casualties. Men were dying all around him. Fane himself was wounded when a bomb burst just in front of his head. Urgent action was needed and he led a desperate dash for a ditch, which would at least give some cover. It soon emerged that only

Superbly equipped German troops pinned down the Glosters at Bois Saint-Acaire. Most had little choice but to surrender. TAYLOR LIBRARY

thirteen men had succeeded in making it with him. Before long they were marching briskly through the darkness with one aim – to get to Dunkirk through enemy lines. Few believed it would be possible and none could have possibly predicted the incredible adventures they would have on the way. Taking cover during the day and guided only by the enemy's red flares, Fane at one point was forced to take a gamble by asking the commander of a German convoy for directions. Amazingly, in the darkness, his uniform was not noticed and they continued their journey to the coast via the village of Oost Cappel, where they broke into a house and feasted on its contents. At one point they rested in a barn and hid under straw bales. Fane recalls:

> *'Soon I began to regret the madness in choosing the barn, for we could hear German voices in the yard outside which gave us some anxiety. In the afternoon some Germans entered the barn and started sorting over the kit in the wagons. We were all paralysed into immobility and I was literally sweating blood all that evening until we could get away.'*

Often they walked perilously close to German troops, many of whom were

Lieutenant Fane

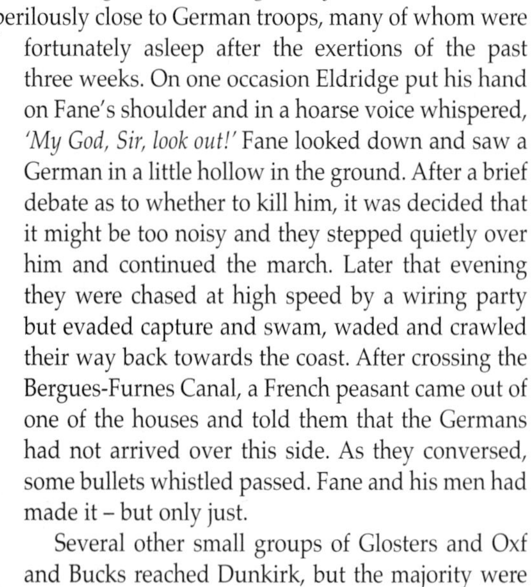

fortunately asleep after the exertions of the past three weeks. On one occasion Eldridge put his hand on Fane's shoulder and in a hoarse voice whispered, *'My God, Sir, look out!'* Fane looked down and saw a German in a little hollow in the ground. After a brief debate as to whether to kill him, it was decided that it might be too noisy and they stepped quietly over him and continued the march. Later that evening they were chased at high speed by a wiring party but evaded capture and swam, waded and crawled their way back towards the coast. After crossing the Bergues-Furnes Canal, a French peasant came out of one of the houses and told them that the Germans had not arrived over this side. As they conversed, some bullets whistled passed. Fane and his men had made it – but only just.

Several other small groups of Glosters and Oxf and Bucks reached Dunkirk, but the majority were either taken prisoner or killed. Their efforts at Cassel were widely acclaimed. Brigadier Somerset was later created CBE not only for his command of the Brigade in the town but also for his work as Senior British Officer in a number of Prisoner of War Camps. Colonel Gilmore's gallant leadership was rewarded with the DSO and other awards included one MC, eleven MMs and one DSC in the Glosters

Glosters subalterns in captivity at Oflag VII B following the fighting around Cassel and Ledringhem, 1940.
Back row: **J. N. Rice, D.B.E. Bilson, R.W. Cresswell, MC.**
Front row: **Private Harris, R. L. Charlesworth, A. Dewsnap, T.S.W. Reeve-Tucker**

alone. Two brave battalions had been decimated but their efforts helped save an entire army.

What To See

The cobbled Grande Place provides a good starting point for a visit to the town. The Tourist Information Centre here has some useful maps of the area. There is a Museum on the southern side of the Place which, although under renovation at the time of the writing of this book, has a good reputation. It was in this building that Foch established his headquarters and there are many photographs, exhibits, weapons and other mementos

Taken by the Germans 30 May 1940 – a corner of Cassel with a German panzer soldier passing a damaged British Tractor 4+4 (Ford FGT).

The same spot some sixty years on.

of the First World War and, to a lesser extent, the Second World War. The history of Cassel is well documented in the Museum and it is worth a visit.

Further down the high street, beside the church, is a corner café called Café aux Trois Moulins. This was the evacuation headquarters in 1940. It is run by Mme Francine Cloet-Vienne, a very friendly French lady, who is only too pleased to talk about the events in 1940. The Glosters' regimental coat of arms adorn either side of the bar. To the left of the café, as you approach it, is the great Northern Gate which faces directly towards Dunkirk. A plaque on the wall in front of it reads:

> *'In proud memory of Brigadier the Hon. N.F. Lawson CBE DSO MC and the 228 officers and men of 2 and 5 Battalions The Gloucestershire Regiment who fought and died from Waterloo to Cassel and Ledringham covering the evacuation of the British and French Forces at Dunkirk 14-29 May 1940.'*

A statue erected in 1928 on the summit of Mont Cassel to honour Maréchal Foch.

To the west of the town, the Place Dunkerque has been renamed the Place du General Vandamme. It was here that the Oxf and Bucks and the Glosters established their headquarters. The local bank where the Glosters were based still exists and is now run by Crédit du Nord. The old Gendarmerie was so damaged by the German artillery bombardments that it was knocked down and replaced by a modern and rather unexciting red bricked building. From the Place du Général Vandamme, it is a short uphill walk to reach Cassel's highest point where a restored 18th century windmill, as well as a fine equestrian statue of Foch, stand. From this vantage point, there are fine views of the surrounding countryside and an incised black stone has arrows pointing to significant locations. It is not hard to imagine how isolated and helpless the defending British soldiers must have felt as they overlooked this panorama with the full knowledge that they were completely surrounded. The Germans made fires at night to reinforce this point further.

I would thoroughly advise any visitor to stop at the cemetery on the eastern side of the town, where there is a Commonwealth War Graves Commission cemetery for Allied soldiers who died in the fighting between 1939-45. Many are members of the Glosters and Oxf and Bucks, including 2/Lieutenant G Weightman who is mentioned earlier in the account of the fighting.

A number of headstones bear Kipling's famous epithet *'Known unto God.'*

Other inscriptions include:

For see! Whereon this bier
Before ye lies
The Fall'n
Th' ultimely sacrifice

And ...

May the joys
He lost on life's journey
Be found
In God's Garden of Peace.

Some have the famous

Greater love hath no man
That he lays down his life for
His friends.

These men's defence of Cassel, in order to buy time for their comrades to evacuate, make such words all the more poignant. Interestingly, there also are a number of graves for Czech soldiers, most of whom died in 1944 when, following D-Day, they prevented the German garrison at Dunkirk from breaking out.

If you have time, you may wish to visit the towns of Bavinchove and Zuytpene. The D933 leads directly to Bavinchove from Cassel, and a right turn at the village's clearly marked crossroads will take you to Zuytpene. I found the two villages, on a gloomy day, rather depressing and lifeless but you might think differently!

The graves of men who paid the ultimate sacrifice attempting to hold back the German attack on Cassel.

Chapter Three

MASSACRE AT ESQUELBECQ

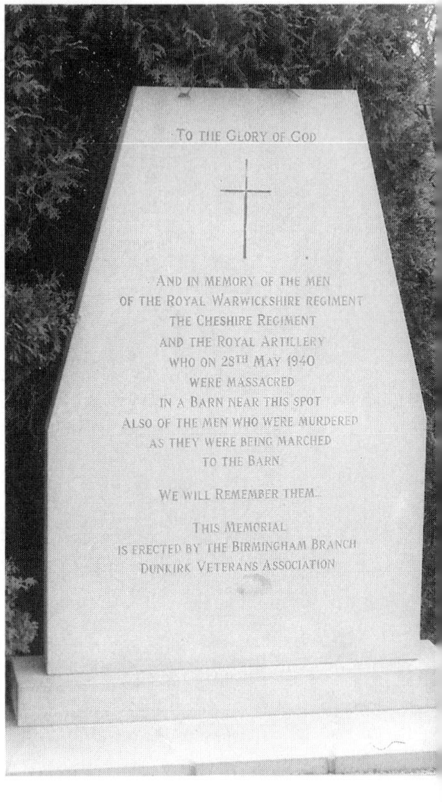

Ten miles north of Cassel on the D916 is the pleasant market town of Wormhoudt. On reaching the town centre, take a turning left on to a minor road signposted for Esquelbecq. This is the road that a number of British soldiers, after a valiant defence of their strongpoints, were marched along as prisoners of war. They were soon to become victims of an infamous massacre perpetrated by their SS captors.

On the left hand side of the road, after some one and a half kilometres, is a sizable white memorial with a flagpole behind it. A large bush now somewhat conceals this from approaching drivers. Opposite the stone is a lay-by for parking your car. This is the first of two memorial plaques to the massacre which has generally been referred to by the name Wormhoudt but which really happened at Esquelbecq. It was dedicated by the Reverend Leslie Aitken, National Chaplain of the Dunkirk Veterans Association, on 28 May 1973, to the victims of this terrible crime. Over two thousand people were present including four survivors of the massacre who had been traced: Charles Daley, Albert Evans, John Lavelle and Alfred Tombs. Their accounts, along with that of Brian Fahey – another survivor, make it possible to retell the story of that fateful day.

Capture

The fighting around Wormhoudt had been fierce for the past two days. The 2nd Battalion, Royal Warwickshire Regiment, along with a number of men from the Cheshire Regiment and the Royal Artillery, had been left to hold up the encircling enemy attack. Their stubborn resistance against a force of massively superior numbers had been heroic but was at last beginning to give way. Facing them was the II Battalion of the *SS*

The Leibstandarte, 2nd Company on the move through France.

Motorcycle reconnaissance troops moving into action.

Leibstandarte Adolf Hitler Division. Originally Hitler's bodyguard, they were crack troops whose fanaticism was matched only by their fighting prowess.

Private Alfred Tombs, positioned by a mound opposite the present day memorial, knew that their situation was hopeless. His platoon had one gun, virtually no ammunition and a few smoke bombs. The morning of the 28th had been relatively quiet, after the fierce fighting of the past few days, but at midday the silence was broken by the ominous rumble of tanks. It became clear that further opposition was futile and they surrendered.

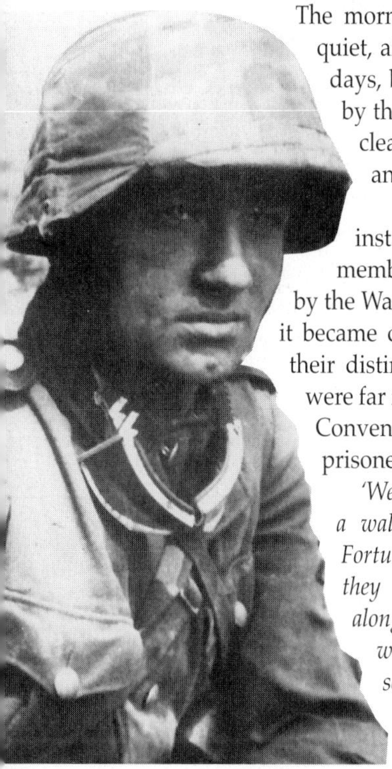

The demeanour of the SS troops instantly disturbed Tombs and the other members of his platoon. Clearly infuriated by the Warwicks' dogged defence of the village, it became clear that these German troops, with their distinctive skull and crossbones insignia, were far from prepared to comply with Geneva Convention mandates on the treatment of prisoners.

'We soon found ourselves lined up against a wall with a machine gun facing us. Fortunately, some rifle fire started up and they called us down. We were marched along a road, where we passed three lorries with the charred bodies of British soldiers inside'.

Brian Fahey, a British Gunner in the 52nd Anti-Tank Regiment, Royal Artillery, was soon to join the fateful march. He had first been alerted that the Germans were approaching when:

'An infantryman came backwards through the hedge, which was screening us. "They're coming down the road," he gasped. The sergeant in charge of my gun said, "Somebody had better go and get the truck," so I made my way round the field keeping my head well down. The lorry driver had problems with the vehicle and, by the time he had got it started, was all ready to go in the opposite direction. "Wait 'til I get the others," I told him. I then hurried back to the gun position but found they had all gone. I was on my own now and, on hearing a truck in the distance, kept down in the ditch fearing it was German. When I saw it was one of our own army lorries, I got up to flag it down. It was hurtling down the road towards me

Retreating British troops ran the gauntlet of enemy ambush.

and was absolutely full of men. The driver and sergeant gestured that they weren't going to stop, so I took the matter into my own hands. I grabbed hold of the struts on the side of the lorry and tried to get a foothold. As it came into the clearing the lorry was hit by everything – a fusillade of rifle and machine gun fire.'

The lorry caught fire and many inside fell victims to the hail of bullets. Fahey, now wounded in the leg, and a few other survivors dropped into the ditch on the side of the road. The lorry soon burned itself out, with ammunition providing a spectacular firework display. Unarmed and wounded, there was little for Fahey to do except wait for the inevitable

9th Company Leibstandarte during the advance through France. TAYLOR LIBRARY

sound of German jackboots.

An hour passed before the Germans arrived, with a party of captives (which included Tombs) that they had rounded up in and around the village. Their mood had not improved and his captors continually prodded Fahey with rifles. Also in this group of around ninety captured men was Charles Daley. His platoon had been in the thick of the action but that afternoon had completely run out of ammunition before being surrounded. The state of his shoulder was further proof of the cowardly behaviour of the SS troops towards their prisoners of war. On surrendering, a German soldier had approached him with a revolver, shouting, *'Engländer Schwein,'* and shot him.

Every man in the group had their own story of how they had been captured. Bert Evans, also in the Warwicks, cursed the fact he had never learnt to swim. He had been taken prisoner as a result of a surprise German attack from the north which had forced his company back towards the river that they had expected would be their buffer. As a non-swimmer, he had been unable to cross it and became one of a number of Warwicks forced to surrender.

The Massacre

It now began to pour with rain as the prisoners were herded off the road and marched across the arable ploughed land about half a mile towards a barn. The swift march at double time proved difficult to sustain across the muddy field and the injured who failed to keep up were continually hit or bayoneted. For Fahey, suffering from a bullet wound in the leg, it was a struggle. He remembered the barn as *'an isolated structure in the middle of the field, a ramshackle, derelict small shed - the kind that cows could go in to get some shelter.'*

As the men were herded in, it became clear that their captors had a far more sinister intention than protection from the torrential rain. Once they were all inside, to their horror the men nearest to the entrance noticed that an SS officer had stopped to pick a hand grenade from his jackboot. Captain Lynn-Allen, who was commanding the Warwicks' D Company and who was the only officer amongst the prisoners, protested against what appeared to be the intention, namely to massacre the prisoners. He also protested that there were a number of wounded, and that the accommodation was insufficient to give them room to lie down. Private Evans takes up the story:

> *'The SS officer, with a twinge of an American accent shouted back, "Yellow Englishman, there will be plenty of room where you're going to". I was standing next to Captain Lynn-Allen, just outside the door of the barn, when the Germans began throwing grenades in. I had my right arm shattered by one of the first explosions. Then, while I was still feeling dazed,*

The barn where 80 to 100 British prisoners were herded and grenades thrown among them. The farm marked with a cross was being used at the time as a temporary HQ for the 2nd Battalion Leibstandarte.

Believed to be a photograph of dead British prisoners gunned down by the SS at the time of the massacre at Wormhout.

> *another grenade was thrown in. Captain Lynn-Allen seized me and dragged me out through the door, while the Germans were taking cover against the explosions. Captain Lynn-Allen practically supported me the whole way until we reached a clump of trees some 200 yards away, where we found a small stagnant pond. We got into it with the water up to our chests. Suddenly, without warning, a German appeared on the bank of the pond just above us. The soldier, who must have spotted us running away, was armed with a revolver and immediately shot Captain Lynn-Allen twice. Captain Lynn-Allen's body fell forward and disappeared under the surface. He then fired at me at a range of about three yards. I was hit twice in the neck and, already bleeding profusely from my arm, I slumped in the water. No doubt he thought that he had finished me off."*

Meanwhile, at the barn, further grenades were thrown in and panic ensued. Tombs remembers dropping to the floor and feeling two men fall on top of him. Some of the bombs were smothered by the heroic action of Sergeant Moore and CSM Jennings, who threw themselves on them and were immediately killed. The situation seemed hopeless. Fahey recalls that, *'Somebody started saying the Lord's Prayer. We were just terrified. My own feeling was one of futility, hopelessness and despair.'*

After a minute or so the SS guards began calling to the prisoners to come out, in fives. Sergeant Garside, of Tombs' platoon, was first to volunteer and, clearly resigned to his fate, left the barn with the words, *'If we've got to go, we've got to go'*. The first five volunteers were then lined up and shot. Fahey volunteered to be one of the next five men to be executed. *'I thought to myself, I can't suffer this any longer. I'm going to go and get it over with.'*

Due to the wound sustained in the lorry ambush, Fahey was carried out by a colleague. Standing away from the barn, with their backs towards the executioners, the five men waited. The firing squad then counted off, *'Eins, zwei, drei, vier, fünf'. 'I was number five. It felt like a punch, like a severe blow, and it just knocked me over.'*

Fahey lay unconscious in the muddy field as the rain continued to pour down. The SS guards, probably because of the conditions, found that execution in fives was too time-consuming. More grenades were thrown into the barn and these were followed by a frenzy of machine gunning. Then, after a while, Private Tombs remembers, it all went quiet, except that, *'One of the lads who was sitting at the back of the barn began screaming "shoot me, shoot me".'*

When Tombs next saw him, he had a bullet through his forehead. With their job completed, and hearing no stirrings in the barn, the SS troops wandered off. Amazingly though, Tombs, blood-soaked and with shrapnel in his leg, found himself alive, as did a few others in the barn. The scene was, however, devastating.

'Kelly was going mad because his leg was blown off in his trousers. He was beating the floor. We went round the others but we couldn't do anything to help them.'

Later that afternoon Tombs and the few in the barn who had miraculously survived the massacre decided to make a run for it. They only got as far as the nearby farmhouse before they were spotted. A cry of 'halt' put an end to their escape. After his ordeal, however, Corporal Box was not prepared to stop and was shot. Fortunately, the German soldiers were not the ones who had been at the barn. Tombs, however, took no chances and avoided mentioning the barn.

Meanwhile, Fahey regained consciousness in the muddy field. The other four men who had been shot with him were not so lucky. He crawled back to the barn to discover the carnage. Fahey particularly remembers:

'One awful thing ... I shall never forget one chap who was sitting up. He was propped against the side of the barn. He'd found a clip of .303 rifle bullets in his pocket and was holding one against his head whilst trying to detonate it with another. I actually prayed that I would be taken because I was so low'.

Fahey stayed in the barn from Tuesday evening to Friday morning.

'The thirst was worse than anything. That's the only effect it (the massacre) had on me for a long, long time. I was terrified, even after the war, of not being able to quench my thirst.'

Fahey was discovered by horrified Wehrmacht troops. They at first assumed that the Warwicks had made a futile last stand. When the incident was explained to them, they replied *'Oh, you must have been captured by the SS. They don't take prisoners.'* For Fahey the war was over and he spent the next five years in a prisoner of war camp.

Bert Evans, who had been shot in the pond, was captured by Wehrmacht stretcher-bearers. His arm was in a terrible state as a result of the grenade attack on the barn. He recalls that, *'A German officer took me to a dressing station. There, maggots were put in my arm to suck up the gangrenous pus.'* Unfortunately the maggots could not save his arm, he was taken to Boulogne and it was amputated under candlelight, whilst he was fully conscious. After three years of captivity Evans was repatriated in a swop of severely wounded and incapacitated prisoners in 1943. The authorities showed little inclination to listen to the story, so he decided to break the news of the massacre to the *Daily Mirror* in October of that year.

Post-War Trials

Whilst it was known that the perpetrators of the killing belonged to II Battalion of the *Leibstandarte SS Adolf Hitler*, no one was brought to trial after the war. The men who carried out the massacre were never identified. Certain things were, however, clear. *SS-Obergruppenführer* Josef Dietrich,

Wilhelm Mohnke

Josef Dietrich

the Commanding Officer of the Regiment, had spent most of the day in a ditch taking cover. As he entered the village, his car came under heavy fire which killed the driver and left Dietrich with little option but to wait for assistance. As a result *SS-Haupsturmführer* Wilhelm Mohnke leading *5 Kompanie* assumed overall command of the regiment through the infamous hours of the massacre.

Both Mohnke and Dietrich survived the war and a case was made out against Mohnke, which accused him of playing a key role in the events at Wormhoudt. The trial was inconclusive as it could not be proven that he had been present at the barn nor was there enough evidence to prove he had ordered, or been aware of, the massacre. This was despite evidence from an SS NCO who claimed that Mohnke was furious that prisoners had been taken, and instructed they should be removed and shot.

In 1988 the massacre achieved greater notoriety when, owing to public pressure, the British government re-opened the case against him. The campaign was such that there was even an appeal for witnesses in some national newspapers. Mohnke who, by this stage was living in retirement in Hamburg, was, however, never brought to trial.

Dietrich escaped any blame for the massacre. However, in 1946 he was sentenced by the US Army for his part in the murder of American prisoners at Malmédy on 17 December 1944. He was released after serving only ten of his twenty-five year sentence, but was promptly imprisoned again for the murders committed on the Night of the Long Knives in 1934, when Ernst Rohm and other leaders of the SA, as well as other political

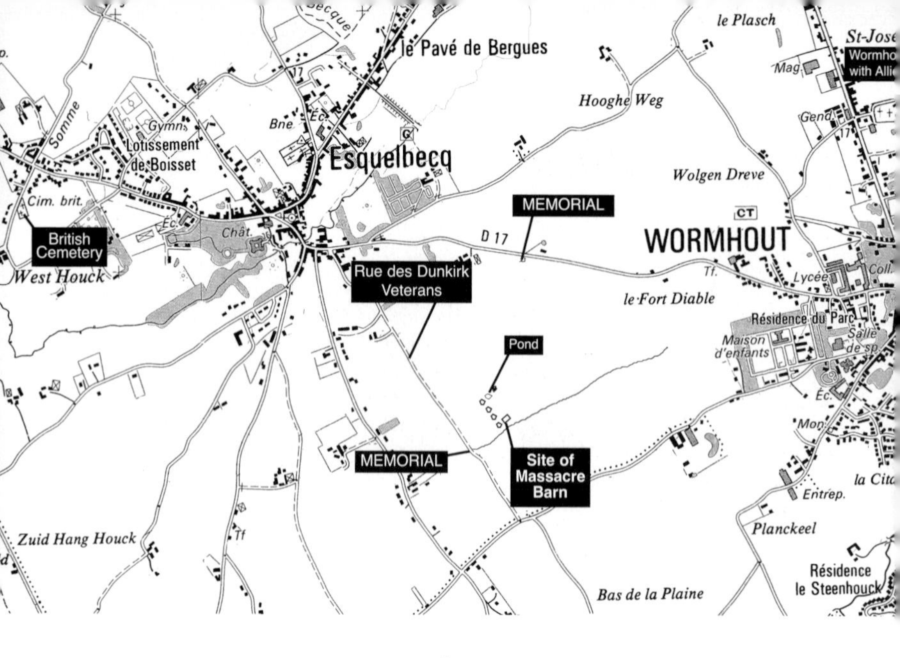

opponents, were executed by the SS.

What To See

Continue on to Esquelbecq and as you enter the village keep your eyes firmly peeled on the left for a rather innocuous blue sign 'Rue Dunkirk Veterans.' If you reach the square you have gone too far. Take this turning and go three-quarters of a mile down a rough unmade but passable track across agricultural land. Park beside the modern brick memorial, built in 1995, which states simply, 'Here the Esquelbecq Massacre took place 28 May 1940.' If you walk some 150 metres along the track to your left towards the line of trees you will reach the 'sacred' tree, where the barn once stood. It is adorned with poppies, nailed wooden crosses, barbed wire, wreaths and coats of arms. Some sixty metres along the line of heavily pollarded willows there is a mound beside the pond that Captain Lynn-Allen and Private Bert Evans escaped to. I found the whole site to be understated and yet highly evocative. Unlike many places, fifty years on, it somehow retains a tragic aura and is a powerful reminder of man's inhumanity to man.

Esquelbecq itself is a quaint village, which is worth a wander around and makes a good coffee stop to revive the spirits after

Left: **The Monument at the end of Rue des Dunkirk Veterens, is a hundred yards from the site of the barn.**

Below: **It was close to this tree that the original barn once stood. It now serves as a shrine where personal tokens of rememberance are attached.**

Bottom: **The pond where Captain Lynn Allen was murdered.**

the emotion of the massacre site. Just out of the village is a cemetery which includes a number of graves for men in the Warwicks. There is also a cemetery at Wormhoudt. It is not clearly marked and you need to look out on the right as you drive out of the town on the D916 back towards Dunkirk. The Commonwealth war graves are at the back left of the civilian cemetery and include 141 British soldiers (most of whom were not victims of the massacre), two airmen and one Indian soldier – 'Groom Akburkham, Royal Indian ASC, Age 24, 22/5/1940.'

Other Massacres During The Withdrawal

The SS troops at Wormhoudt were not alone in committing acts of atrocity. The *SS Totenkopf* soon developed a reputation as the most evil German division in France at this time. It had been responsible for a number of massacres around the Arras sector, including the shooting of twenty-three civilian hostages at the Hermant Farm in Pont-du-By on 23 May, ninety-eight others in and near Aubigny, and forty-five at Vandelicourt. Yet, it was its actions at the village of Le Paradis which gained most infamy.

The victims were men in the 2/Royal Norfolks who had been fighting a desperate rearguard action for the past 36 hours. By the afternoon on 27

Men of the *Totenkopf* during the fighting.

British casualties.

May, exhausted and depleted, these soldiers had endured incessant enemy assaults and bombardments. The situation had become hopeless. Headquarter Company, cut off and desperately short of ammunition, were left with little option but to surrender. Their SS captors, who had earlier that day lost their Regimental Commander in the fighting, then marched them towards a meadow nearby. To their horror, on reaching it the Norfolks noticed two heavy machine guns pointing in their direction. Under the supervision of their commander, Fritz Knoechlein, No 3 Company of the 1st Battalion 2nd *SS Totenkopf* had carefully premeditated the murder of the men who had so frustrated their advance. The machine guns opened up and for a few seconds the cries and shrieks drowned the sound of their murderous fire. When the shooting stopped, Knoechlein's troops finished the job with either bayonet or bullet.

Of the ninety-nine Norfolks that had been captured, only two survived. One of these was Signaller Pooley who, despite being shot twice in the leg, kept perfectly still, feigning death, and survived. Signaller Callaghan was also alive as a result of lying beneath the corpses of his fallen colleagues.

Later the bodies were discovered by an elderly aristocratic German officer, Major Friedkerr von Riedner. He was horrified and promptly reported the scene to army headquarters.

> *'These people had almost all suffered head wounds from shots that must have been fired at close range. Some had their whole skull smashed in, an injury that can almost only be caused by a blow from a gun butt or similar means.'*

An enquiry was made but came to nothing. The SS claimed that the

Norfolks had used soft-nosed dum-dum bullets, contrary to the Geneva Convention and had hung out swastikas to lure German troops into an ambush.

The massacre at Le Paradis, unlike that of Wormhoudt, did at least result in the perpetrators coming to justice. Signaller Pooley, who had sworn during the murders to exact revenge on those responsible, got his wish and his evidence was vital in Knoechlein's trial. He was found guilty and hanged on 29 January 1949.

Both sides committed war crimes and merely to cite the SS would be an injustice. At Vinch in Belgium Wehrmacht troops summarily shot eighty-six civilians. There were also a number of incidents in which Allied troops shot German prisoners. When, for example, a Heinkel He 111 crash-landed in a field at Vimy on 18 May British and French soldiers murdered the surrendering airmen as they tumbled out of the wreck with their hands up. Such crimes were later investigated by the German authorities. The Heinkel crash enquiry was typical and many locals were arrested. Possession of pieces from the aircraft meant almost certain execution.

Fighting on other strongpoints

Gort's strongpoints were only as effective as the men defending them. The fact that they have been viewed, in hindsight, as such a vital factor in

Rudder fin from an Heinkel 111 brought down in France. The German crew from a shot-down Heinkel were gunned down by British and French soldiers as they tried to surrender.

the success of 'Dunkirk' is testament to the incredible fighting spirit and selflessness of the regiments charged with holding them. It was not just at Cassel and Wormhoudt that the British troops excelled. The 2/Dorsets' defiant defence of Festubert and the valiant efforts of 1/Buckinghamshire Battalion to hold out at Hazebrouck were mirrored by troops throughout all Gort's stops. Indeed the two epic actions at Merville and La Bassée would warrant mention in any military annals.

Britain's oldest regiment, The Royal Scots, under Lieutenant Colonel Money were positioned on the crossing over the River Lys. On 27 May the men of the 2nd *Waffen SS* launched an especially ferocious assault from a wood on their western flank. It was not long before the Royal Scots were suffering high casualties from the intense rifle and mortar fire. Direct hits on three trucks containing ammunition in the yard opposite a Company Headquarters killed a number of men, as they had to run past the vehicles to escape. Things went from bad to worse when their advanced dressing station was overrun. A German NCO, who claimed the Royal Scots were using dum-dum bullets, was only just persuaded not to kill the wounded by the pleas of a Chaplain, the Reverend Norman McClean.

Soon fighting was occurring on every part of the line. Battalion Headquarters, defended by clerks, cooks, drivers and stretcher-bearers, provided stout resistance, but the flames in the building forced them to abandon their position. In the meantime the Germans were systematically mopping up the last areas of resistance. Major Bruce, who had taken over command when Lieutenant Colonel Money became a casualty, escaped with a few survivors on to a hillside, where they attacked travelling German lorries. Unfortunately their presence was revealed to the enemy by a local and they were captured. The Royal Scots' last stand at Merville had been a heroic one, but had resulted in only a few remnants of this famous Battalion ever reaching Dunkirk.

The 1/Queen's Own Cameron Highlanders also showed exceptional tenacity defending La Bassée, the southern anchor of Gort's strongpoint system. After deciding to stay and fight to the last, they held out for two days against massively superior forces. They paid a heavy price for their bravery. After one counter-attack A Company (normally 130) was left with six men. Indeed only one hundred Camerons survived the ferocious fighting that occurred between 26-28 May.

Some days after the battle at La Bassée, Stanley Allen, a British rating aboard HMS *Windsor* was embarking troops off the Dunkirk mole. A file of Scottish soldiers wearing khaki aprons over their kilts and led by an officer with his arm in a sling approached the ship.

> *'The wounded Scottish officer called out to the bridge, "What part of France are you taking us to?" One of the naval officers replied, "We're taking you back to Dover". The Scotsmen were disgusted and said they*

Some of the one hundred survivors of the 1/Queen's Own Cameron Highlanders going into captivity. They chose to fight on rather than be evacuated.

were not bloody well coming. They promptly turned round and went back to continue the war with the Germans on their own. It really was remarkable.'

As the Highlanders were the only regiment in the BEF still to be wearing the kilt, there can be no doubt that these were the very men involved in the action at La Bassée. Twenty-one of the one hundred survivors remained on the perimeter to the last, and the regiment, which used to be known as the 79th Foot, left Dunkirk with only seventy-nine men to show for its supreme efforts.

The actions at Le Paradis, Festubert, Hazebrouck, La Bassée, Merville and all the other strongpoints enabled the battered troops of the BEF to move up the sixty mile escape corridor.

The Escape Corridor

Once defence of these 'stops' became untenable, the troops occupying them attempted to join the throng of soldiers making their way to the port and beaches through narrow corridors. Every man who made this journey has his own story, but all agree that the desperate withdrawal to the coast was a humiliating and often harrowing experience. Leonard Howard, an NCO in the Royal Engineers, was one of these soldiers:

'It was a case of every man for himself. The scene was pretty chaotic. The Germans were very close and people were being killed all around you. At 21 years old, I hadn't experienced death before. Survival, of course, was the main object in everyone's mind. I remember a Regimental Sergeant Major walking down the road. Tears were streaming down his face and he said, "I never thought I would see the British Army like this". The poor man was absolutely shattered.'

All too often military transport was lacking and troops used any means possible to get back. The sight of soldiers on stolen bicycles was not uncommon. There were even sightings of individuals on roller-skates. Charles Williams, a wireless operator, recalls riding a horse back to Dunkirk:

'I came across a field with French cavalry horses in it and saddles and bridles dumped there also. I caught a chestnut horse, saddled up, mounted and continued my way following the crowded road. I was part of a mass exodus. However, being of the Royal Horse Artillery tradition, pre-war, I soon overtook my erstwhile comrades along the way! Inevitably I was ordered by an officer to dismount but, in view of the state of my feet, I ignored his order and promptly trotted off in the direction of Dunkirk.'

For most, it was a long and exhausting trek on foot. Blisters were a common complaint. Private Fred Clapham in the Durham Light Infantry remembers other walking ailments:

'The weather was very hot and sunny all the time that we were walking to the coast. As we were all wearing army issue woollen "long johns" our crotches were all sore with constant rubbing of the garments and perspiration. Consequently after a few days, we were marching with our legs as far apart as we could, officers included... It must have looked quite comical.'

To add to their problems, many units had run out of rations and were forced to use their own initiative. Farms were often a welcome source of nourishment for soldiers, even if their hosts were less than pleased to see them. By this stage their inhabitants would have known that, wherever the BEF were, the Germans would be in close pursuit. Discarded lorries were sometimes loaded with unexpected goods. On the whole, though, most went hungry and thirsty. Some like Frank Shearman, in the Royal Army Ordnance Corps, found their search for food led to unusual situations:

'Everyone scrounged what food they could. We came to a farm where a herd of cows were frantic with pain, as their udders were so full. No one knew how to milk a cow and they tried with two men holding the cow's head whilst two more tried the milking! In fact the animals went berserk and had to be shot'

All too often there was little time to even contemplate food with the Germans so close behind. At times soldiers found the enemy between them and the coast and were forced to run the gauntlet of passing them. Leon Stribly had one particularly close encounter:

'We mostly sheltered under hedgerows or where there was any cover by day, and walked at night. The Germans kept passing by. On one occasion we had to take shelter in a farmyard, so we climbed up on top of a stack of baled straw in the middle of the yard area. The Germans went round our stack several times and then questioned the farmer at the farmhouse. He

must have known we were there, as when we arrived a light went out in his house. But the Germans departed. It was a narrow escape.'

Some, like Leonard Howard, were not so lucky and were forced into skirmishes with the enemy. His unit suffered a great number of casualties, being constantly hounded by the Germans during their withdrawal. Not only had they suffered intense mortaring and machine-gunning, but they were also victim of three ambushes. He particularly remembers one of these incidents due to the bravery shown by a friend:

'At one stage on our trek from Fletre to Dunkirk, enemy machine-gun fire had us completely pinned down. We really were suffering a terrific amount of casualties. A good cricketing mate of mine, George Parks, stood up and threw a Mills grenade through the loophole on this pillbox, which was knocking hell out of us. Somehow he wasn't shot. I was laying on the deck - so was anyone else with any sense and he just said, "How's that for a cricket throw?" He got a Military Medal for it. It was one of the bravest things I saw.'

Throughout the dash to the coast the men tried if possible to walk through fields rather than on roads. This was partly due to the state of the refugees who slowed the soldiers down. Even in the last days of May the Stukas targeted these innocent victims of war, as they had in Belgium, and to mingle with them was generally deemed unsafe. For many, the situation on the main highways was simply too depressing. Arthur Gunn was particularly shocked at one sight:

'There was a dead young mother lying on the road with a baby still suckling her breast. We gave the baby to another young woman who had a child with her.'

There was little time to ponder on the horror of such scenes. The exhausted troops just had to make their way towards the black smoke that identified the town of Dunkirk.

British troops arriving inside the Dunkirk perimeter.

CHAPTER FOUR

DEFENCE OF THE PERIMETER

The Perimeter

The Allied leaders were well aware that the strongpoints would not be able to hold out for ever. On 27 May General Adam, appointed by Gort to organize the evacuation, arranged a meeting with key British and French commanders to hammer out an effective strategy for defending the beachhead. During the course of the morning, the general layout of the Dunkirk perimeter was agreed. The French would be responsible for the line west of Dunkirk, the BEF for everything east. It was twenty-five miles wide and up to eight miles deep, covering all evacuation points from La Panne to the beaches past the Dunkirk harbour. The Allied leaders made the most of the local waterways with the British sector running along the canal from Bergues to Furnes and then finally to Nieuport.

The man who was charged with the awesome responsibility of commanding this defensive line was Brigadier the Honourable E.F. Lawson. His first job was to try and deploy as many men as possible to man the perimeter. It was no easy task as it involved ordering exhausted men, many of whom had been in the thick of the fighting for weeks, to sacrifice their hopes of imminent embarkation. At first he was forced to pluck troops from the beaches, later he would be able to use the men

In hot pursuit – a 3.7cm Pak 35/36 anti-tank gun and crew. This weapon was dubbed 'the door knocker' by its operators, as its shells failed to penetrate all but the weakest armour.

streaming down the escape corridor. The fact that within twenty-four hours a defensive ring had been achieved is testament to both Lawson's leadership and the British soldiers' fighting spirit.

The men forming this shield needed little reminding that their efforts were vital to the success or failure of 'Operation Dynamo'. Many must have known that they had forfeited their chances of rescue and, yet, through their actions, they allowed many more men to evacuate than anyone had dreamed possible. Rarely has such sacrifice for one's fellow man been so much in evidence.

Bergues

Bergues is some 10 kilometres north of Wormhoudt on the D916 and its ancient walled fortifications make it easily recognizable from the road. Simply follow the signs into the town. Once you have crossed the moat and passed through the impressive Bergues Gate, the directions for the town centre are self-explanatory by any standards. It is a beautiful old town, which has recovered remarkably well since its siege in 1940. The charming market square is the town's focal point. Situated here is the impressive

The town of Bergues was a key point strongpoint in the defence of the Dunkirk perimeter.

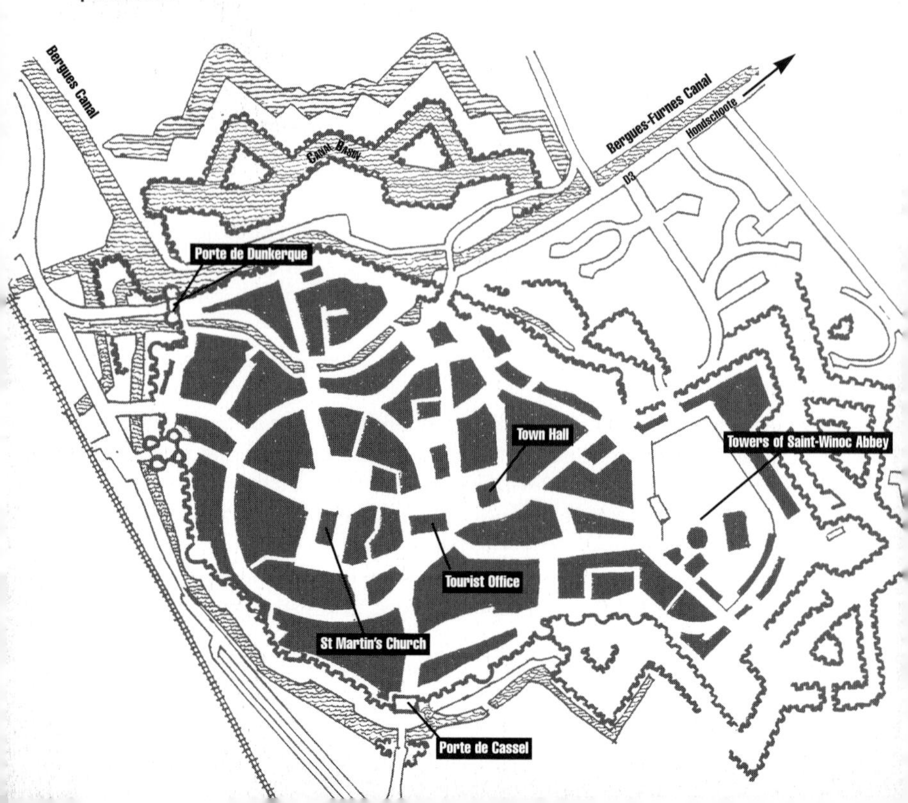

Church of Saint Winoc, badly damaged during the fighting, which has been lovingly restored since. For an understanding of Bergues' early history, as well as for getting useful maps and guides, it is well worth visiting the Tourist Information Centre which is in the base of the church. There are plenty of cafés and restaurants which, along with its peaceful and relaxed atmosphere, make Bergues an ideal stopping place on your tour. There is little evidence now of the devastation caused by artillery and air attacks as the Germans desperately tried to seize this key defensive site during the period 28 May - 2 June 1940.

The many soldiers who made their way through this ancient fortified town as they headed towards Dunkirk have one common recollection - vehicles. It is hard to imagine as you drive towards Bergues that in late May 1940 it was strewn with a mass of destroyed British transport, lined up against hedges and in the ditches on the side of the road, all the way to the port itself. The abandonment of vehicles on entering the perimeter was aimed at easing the congestion problems. Major James Moulton of GHQ recalls:

> *'We set up points at which vehicles were stopped. Before long there was a queue, sometimes three deep, going all the way out past Bergues. I remember thinking "I don't know what's going to happen if this lot come under attack". When I next came back they had been attacked and there were only a few clumps.'*

Where the Stukas failed to destroy the transport, the British did so themselves. Charles Nash, a NCO with Royal Army Service Corps, observed this in action:

> *'We were told to leave our lorry. There were hundreds of other vehicles*

Discarded British vehicles were deliberately vandalized so as to render them useless.

Abandoned equipment bears testimony to an army in desperate plight. TAYLOR LIBRARY

and these were all dealt with by a gang of Engineers - brutalizing the vehicles, punching petrol tanks and doing certain things under the engines to render them useless to the enemy.'

Such a policy made complete sense but hardly improved the morale of the retreating soldiers, who viewed this depressing welcome into the perimeter as yet another reminder of the terrible plight the BEF now found itself facing. Looting of these vehicles was commonplace and did at least perk up a number of flagging spirits, as soldiers crammed goods in their haversacks and webbing. When Major Edward Poulton of the Royal Fusiliers, positioned on the edge of the perimeter asked a sergeant for a cigarette, he was surprised to have a two hundred carton pressed on him. 'No, no, keep some for yourself – I'll have two packets,' Poulton insisted. The sergeant promptly replied, 'Keep the carton, sir, I've got ten thousand.'

From Tuesday 28 May the numbers of troops making their way through the town reduced dramatically. For the Loyal Regiment, who had the unenviable task of manning defences around the 17th century-old walls surrounding Bergues, this could mean only one thing – the Germans were nearby. Sure enough, at dawn the next day a massive bombardment was unleashed on the town, which continued for the next three days.

By Friday, 31 May the British defenders faced not only murderous shelling but also enemy ground assaults as well. Lieutenant Colonel John Sandie, the Loyals' Commanding Officer, with only twenty-six officers and

451 men as well as some other 'odds and sods' from other Regiments, was aware that his troops would be unable to keep the enemy out for much longer. Against massively superior numbers, the fact that they had held the Germans up for so long was in itself a triumph of nerve and spirit. However, the Bergues garrison, which even included a company of ex-London bus drivers, continued their dogged defence throughout the day. Indeed, according to General Pownall later, a posse of padres led by the Reverend Alfred Naylor held the bridge at Bergues throughout this time and did sterling work questioning suspect fifth columnists too.

Cassel Gate at Bergues was a key point on the Dunkirk perimeter. During the defence this gate was blocked by a bulldozer.

The locals also played their part. One example of this was at Steene, south-west of the town, where General von Kleist's tanks tried to prise an opening. In a desperate attempt to resist their advance, Mayor Jean Duriez, an industrial manufacturer, turned the faucets of ten vast stills to send two million gallons of raw spirits gushing across the countryside. To his astonishment, an artillery shell exploded nearby turning the flooded fields into a raging sea of flame. Trapped by the inferno that engulfed them, two of von Kleist's tanks glowed white hot. The advance from the west was, for the time being, stalled.

Fires were raging in Bergues itself, making life desperately uncomfortable for the troops dug in around the ancient ramparts. Black viscous smoke filled the air and despatch riders could only grope through it on foot, with mouths and noses bound with damp cloths. Exhausted but undeterred by these terrible conditions, the Loyals stayed put.

The Bergues – Furnes Canal

It is now time to leave the fortress town of Bergues and visit other areas of the perimeter which saw desperate fighting and many deeds of valour by the hard-pressed defenders.

Making your way out of the town, pick up the D3 and head east for approximately three kilometres until you reach Hoymille. You will notice that the Bergues-Furnes canal is, as it was in 1940, a formidable obstacle, being some 15-20 metres wide with steep banks. For the hard pressed BEF this was a heaven-sent defensive line in what was otherwise open country,

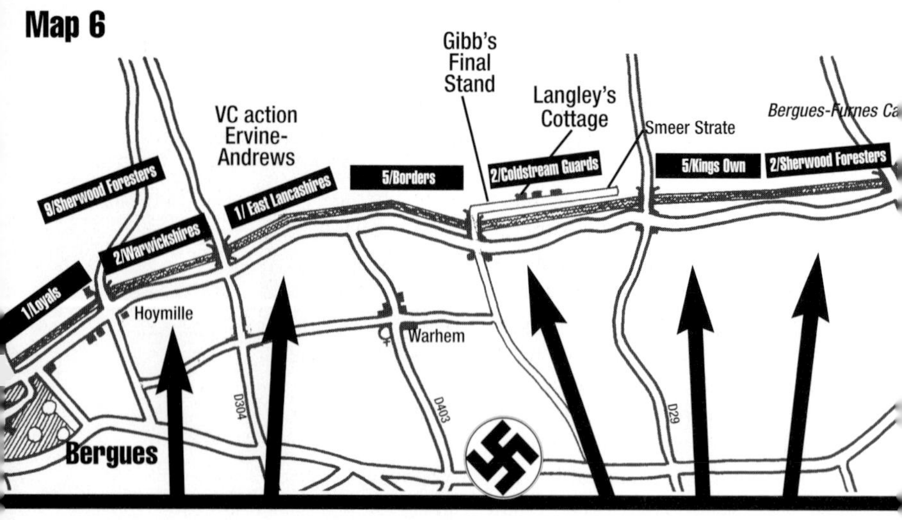

Situation on Bergues-Furnes Canal: British defensive positions and German thrusts.

offering easy going for the German Panzers and infantry.

As you pass through Hoymille, you enter the sector occupied by the 1/East Lancashires and it was here that the first Victoria Cross of the Second World War was to be won. Further along this road you will reach the sector manned by the Coldstream Guards, whose heroic action will also be covered.

The German Offensive

On Saturday, 1 June the Germans deployed a massive four divisions against the six thinly spread battalions on this canal, running east of Bergues. That the British defenders would eventually succumb to the enemy was inevitable, the issue was, for how many hours they could hold out? The men they were fighting against not only had superior numbers

Light tanks Pz Mks I and II enter a burning village.

and plentiful weapons and ammunition, they were also battle-hardened troops who had displayed great soldiering over the past three weeks. The one consolation for the British was that the forces they faced, like themselves, had been desperately hard used by this time. The German 14th and 18th Divisions, for instance, had already been heavily involved in the fighting on the Dyle and the Escaut as well as at Ypres.

The battle began at 5.00am with an attack and heavy bombardment on Tetegham to the north-east of Bergues. The 1/East Lancashires and a company of Royal Warwicks on their right, whose frontage included the bridge at Hoymille, bore the brunt of this fierce assault. The Warwicks, whilst putting up a valiant defensive action, were slowly driven back, having inflicted substantial German casualties. The enemy, sometimes swimming, gradually managed to establish positions across the canal.

Brigadier Constable, whose 139 Brigade was responsible for this sector of the line, rapidly concluded that the Germans had to be prevented from forming an effective foothold on the Allied side of the canal if the perimeter was not to be terminally breached. The problem was that more than just his reserves, comprising seventy men of the 2/5 Leicesters would be required to stem the offensive. He therefore ordered the 1/Loyals to evacuate Bergues and counter-attack in order to push the Germans back to the other side of the canal. Unfortunately the Loyals, who had somehow endured the heavy bombardments directed on the town for the past few days relatively unscathed, suffered appalling losses as they left the town. One shell alone killed nine men and wounded seventeen others. When their counter-attack was finally made, the Loyals found themselves severely hampered by the terrible fighting conditions. Knee-deep in water and with little cover from machine-gun fire, their first assault was a desperate failure. Undeterred, they fought on and, with the aid of some of the Inniskillings' light tanks, succeeded in finding a position that prevented further crossings, although failing to push all the Germans back to the other side of the canal.

A little further along the line, marks where the East Lancashire Regiment attempted to resist a further heavy German attack. Their right flank, in particular was in serious danger of collapsing against strong pressure from advanced units of the German 20th Motorized Division. The story of the desperate defence is an epic one and, from it, a hero emerged to save the day.

Captain Ervine-Andrews VC and the East Lancashires

For the exhausted men of the East Lancashire Regiment, it was almost the end of their long journey to the coast. Dunkirk loomed on the horizon and with it their hopes of returning to England. Their withdrawal had been an eventful one ever since leaving Armentières and the Battalion had suffered a number of casualties fighting rearguard actions on the way. On reaching the perimeter all vehicles were destroyed, seemingly signifying the end of their adventure. Yet hopes of embarkation were soon shattered with the arrival of a Staff Officer from Divisional Headquarters who, realizing they were a complete fighting unit, informed them that perimeter defences urgently required well-organized and properly led troops. Evacuation would have to wait.

Instructions were soon received to move back up the Bergues-Furnes Canal, where they were to take a position near the village of Galghoek. On their right was the company of Warwicks and, on their left, the 2/Coldstream Guards. Their orders were simple – to let no German pass their 1,000-yard frontage. The low-lying ground had been deliberately flooded by opening the sluice gates a month earlier and this aided the defenders as it would inevitably hamper the speed at which the Germans could attack. Indeed, to break through the enemy would be forced to not only wade but to swim in places. The disadvantage of this flooding was that it made life far from comfortable for the British defenders. Often the only refuge from the water were the top floors of the various farmsteads scattered around.

Morale remained high but their predicament was far from enviable. It was only a matter of time before the might of the Wehrmacht would be upon them. The odds seemed stacked against them not only because they lacked sufficient manpower to sustain a defence, but also due to a desperate shortage of firepower. Captain Harold Marcus Ervine-Andrews, Commanding B Company, had discovered the latter over two weeks before at Tournai:

> *'I was asked how many anti-tank mines I required. In my innocence, I replied "Five hundred" to which the reply came back, "Well, the Regiment's got fifty and you're not getting any".'*

By the time they had reached the perimeter stocks were even more depleted and the little equipment and weaponry they did have was deemed substandard.

> *'We were very, very sore that we didn't have bigger anti-tank defences. My biggest anti-tank gun was a 0.5 AT rifle – very effective with a soft-nose bullet against an elephant, but not capable of taking on a large tank.'*

The only rations and ammunition available were those carried by the men themselves. Artillery support was negligible and, with the exception of a few carriers, all the transport had been abandoned. To make matters worse, no forms of communication existed except by way of despatch drivers who used salvaged motorcycles.

On the morning of 31 May the enemy attacked in numbers but the East Lancs' forward companies effectively repelled every assault. At nightfall casualties were evacuated and A and B Companies then replaced their exhausted colleagues on the frontline. Captain Ervine-Andrews recalled:

'We knew we were in for a big attack the next day because D Company, who we were replacing had been having it pretty hard... At dawn on 1 June, the enemy attacked. There was a tremendous barrage of artillery and mortaring throughout the first attack. It must have gone on for two to three hours.'

Barns were set alight with incendiary bullets and buildings were smashed by the intensity of the bombardment, but the Lancashires held their ground.

'During the course of the morning most of my four positions were pretty all right – the odd casualty here and there, but one position was in desperate straits. They were running very short of ammunition and were forced to search the dead bodies in order to find some more.'

Captain Harold Ervine-Andrews VC

The situation soon became critical elsewhere, with casualties mounting and with both his flanks now being threatened. Second Lieutenant Griffin, whose courage in this action was rewarded with a Military Cross, ran the gauntlet of heavy bombardment and murderous machine-gun fire to supply B Company with three Bren carriers and a precious supply of ammunition. This eased the situation and the men were now able to consolidate their defences and continue resistance. However, by mid-morning their fortunes changed yet again with another determined German assault. Word reached Ervine-Andrews that one of his forward positions was in serious danger of being overrun. Their machine-gun had jammed and waves of attacking troops were getting dangerously near.

'One of my sections had a tremendous onslaught on them and was in a very, very bad way. They now asked for urgent help. I had no reserves whatsoever. I picked up my rifle and some ammunition and, looking at the

Looking north to where the VC action took place. The barn was situated in the field close to where this tributary joins the canal.

few soldiers with me in Company Headquarters, said "I'm going up. Who's coming with me?" Every single man came forward.'

The section that needed relief was situated in an exposed barn, where a small tributary outlet joins the Bergues canal. The roof was already ablaze when the Captain and his men, having endured heavy fire to reach it, finally got there. From the blazing rafters, Ervine-Andrews took control of the situation with complete disregard for his own safety. He was well known in his Battalion as a good shot and, in order to save previous ammunition, ordered his men to do little shooting themselves. He later explained his tactics during the battle:

'My men didn't fire much because we were too short of ammunition. They realized it was better that I should do the firing rather than waste the few bullets we had. If you fire accurately and hit men, then the others get discouraged. It's when you fire a lot of ammunition and don't do any damage that the other chaps start being very brave and push on. When they're suffering severe casualties, they are inclined to stop or, in this case, move round to the flanks.'

Ervine-Andrews soon proved that his reputation as an accomplished marksman was well deserved. With the low-lying terrain providing little cover for the enemy, he had an excellent field of fire and he used it to deadly effect. He picked off no fewer than seventeen Germans with his rifle in terribly adverse circumstances. The din was terrific and around five hundred shells were falling every hour in the vicinity, as well as an estimated forty mortar bombs a minute. Heavy-machine gun fire also added to the mayhem and casualties inevitably mounted. Throughout this time Ervine-Andrews supervised the evacuation of the wounded on two of the Bren carriers and was still exercising overall command of his company. Meanwhile, his men in the barn managed to repair the Bren gun, which he then proceeded to fire from his shoulder. Further accurate fire allowed him to dominate the entire thousand-yard sector.

At various points, though, the Germans did get desperately close to reaching the barn and his men, often without weapons, were forced to use any means possible to prevent the enemy taking it. Private John Taylor recalls, *'It was a right do – when the ammo ran low, we kicked, choked, even bit them."* Throughout these bloodstained minutes, no German ever broke the line and gradually they fell back in confusion.

During a lull in the fighting, sometime around three o'clock in the afternoon, Ervine-Andrews ordered his Second-in-Command, Lieutenant F.O. Cetre to return to the Battalion Headquarters and report that their situation would soon become untenable without further supplies of ammunition. Cetre, returning with a small party of men and a fresh supply of ammunition, passed a message from HQ that Ervine-Andrews was to hold his positions until the last round and then withdraw. For his part in the Galghoek action Cetre received the Military Cross.

By early evening the last round had been fired and it was time to pull out. For some ten hours the German advance on this front had been halted by Ervine-Andrews and his men, thus enabling the rest of their Battalion to withdraw and regroup on the Canal des Chats. A new dilemma now faced them:

> *'I had two wounded men. My intention was to tell them to stay at the barn because the Germans could look after them better than we could. However, they said they wanted to be evacuated so we put them on the Bren*

From a painting of the action in which Captain Ervine-Andrews won the VC by John Walton RA.

carrier that we'd kept for ourselves. My men accepted the decision with no qualms.'

This was an act of supreme selflessness on the part of Ervine-Andrews and the eight remaining soldiers of B Company, as they now had no means of transport to withdraw on. It was still daylight and they had little option but to wade and swim their way back along the minor waterways and canals to the coast while often under enemy fire. They reached the beaches on the morning of 3 June, where they were lifted off by one of the small boats which ferried them to the destroyer *Shikhari,* on one of the last of the organized evacuation runs.

Later that month the Battalion learnt that a number of B Company had been awarded decorations for their part in the defence of the canal. Among these were a DCM for the Sergeant Major and a Military Medal for one of the privates. There was, however, no mention made of Captain Ervine-Andrews who had always insisted that it was a company action. A few weeks later he discovered he had been awarded the Victoria Cross. News of this came 'like a bolt out of the blue' to the recipient: 'I was sitting in a West End restaurant when it was announced on the nine o'clock news. It left me completely shaken and surprised.'

To his amazement, Ervine-Andrews became a hero overnight. The story of his valiant action captured the public imagination at the time when good news stories about the war were few and far between. Journalists had a field day. Pictures of the only man to achieve such an honour during the fighting at Dunkirk were carried by every newspaper. The children's magazine *The Victor* even covered the story in a two-page cartoon strip.

To the last Ervine-Andrews was embarrassed by the huge public recognition of his efforts. In a speech at Stonyhurst, he told the boys:

'Anything that I was able to achieve was made possible by the support and bravery of my men.'

His citation is, however, probably closer to the truth:

'His magnificent example imbued his own troops with the dauntless fighting spirit which he himself displayed.'

The Coldstream Guards Defence 'At All Costs'

The fierce defence of the East Lancs had led to the Germans attempting to outflank them. The 5/Borders on their left bore the brunt of this change of tactic and they incurred heavy casualties. After hard fighting they were forced back to the Canal des Chats, thus exposing the right flank of 2/Coldstream Guards.

The Coldstreams had been in position since 29 May with a front covering 2,200 yards. Their orders were to hold the line until 10 o'clock in the evening on 1 June. Like the East Lancs, the Coldstreams had expected their withdrawal to end at Dunkirk, but their hopes were shattered by an announcement from Brigadier Beckwith-Smith's ('Becky' to all) who commanded 1st Guards Brigade.

'Marvellous news. The best ever. It is splendid, absolutely splendid. We have been given the supreme honour of being the rear-guard at Dunkirk.'

While many may not have found it quite such exciting news, the officers noted that his high spirits and enthusiasm were infectious and seemed to imbue the guardsmen with optimism as they braced themselves for the impending German onslaught.

Walking along their front, it is easy to see why the Battalion War Diary describes it as an excellent defensive position. The flat ground provided a superb field of fire and the troops made every possible use of the cottages around them. They presumed, rightly as it transpired, that the Germans would attack first rather than systematically destroy any buildings in the area that they suspected might be a strong-point. Tired though the Guards were, trench systems were dug along the canal bank.

By evening of 29 May the depleted Battalion, with a strength of little more than 200, were in position. 1 Company was on the right, covering the smaller of the two bridges, 3 Company in the centre, 2 and 4 covering the main bridge on the left. 1 Company's headquarters was in a trench; 2 and 3 Companies had theirs in cottages standing back from the canal; No 4 was in a farm-house off the road running back to Krommelhoek; and it was at Krommelhoek, in a windmill just off the road, that Battalion Headquarters was established.

Positions behind the Canal held by the Guards.

German artillery laying down fire into the defensive perimeter.

After investigation, it seems this is 'Langley's Cottage'.

Lieutenant Jimmy Langley

Lieutenant Jimmy Langley and a number of 3 Company were positioned in a large Flemish farm cottage where, as the story of the Coldstream's defence unfolds, much heroic fighting occurred. Neither the roof nor the end walls were really strong enough, but two excellent Bren gun nests were constructed in the attic with the aid of some pieces of old furniture and several crates of empty beer bottles. The removal of some roof tiles aided observation.

As the Guardsmen waited, they saw a procession of stragglers – all on foot, as no transport except ambulances was allowed to cross the canal stream over the bridges and through the Battalions' position to the coast. Jimmy Langley recalls some outstanding individuals making their way to the coast:

'One, a corporal in the Royal East Kents ('Buffs'), particularly excited my admiration. Barely five feet tall, wearing socks, boots and trousers held up by string, he had a Bren gun slung on each shoulder with a rifle strung across their barrels. The slings of the Bren guns had cut deep into his shoulders, his back and chest were caked with blood and I could see part of both his collarbones. I offered him a mug of tea and ordered him

to drop the Bren guns as I would be needing them. He looked me up and down. "I would rather take them with me, Sir." I told him to obey orders but he still made no effort to comply. Instead, in a tired and utterly unemotional voice, gazing over my shoulder, he spoke his mind. "My major's dead somewhere back there. His last words were 'Get those guns back to England, they will be needing them soon.'" He looked me straight in the eyes, "And begging your pardon, Sir, I am going to." I put a generous measure of whisky in his tea, a first-aid dressing between the slings and his shoulders and wished him the best of luck.'

Less impressive was the conduct of some of the French soldiers who passed by. Many threw their weapons in the canal and, when remonstrations ensued, they simply shrugged their shoulders, stating that France had lost the war and that surrender was the only course of action left open to them. A number of Coldstreams were also angered by the conduct of the French officers, who repeatedly told them that they were stupid fools to carry on fighting. Such thoughts no doubt crossed their own minds, but, with the splendid haul of ammunition, the Battalion had acquired from the abandoned lorries, along with decent defensive positions, all were confident that they could at least put up a good fight. Langley's diary, for instance, noted that his Company comprised only thirty-seven men had twelve Bren guns, three Lewis guns, one Boyes anti-tank rifle, 30,000 rounds of small arms ammunition and twenty-two Mills grenades. Such an arsenal instilled confidence in the same way that their enormous food supplies helped raise morale. Indeed, if, as Napoleon once stated, an 'army marches on its stomach', then the Coldstreams could have made their way across most of Europe. No. 3 Company's cottage Headquarters resembled 'a small country grocer's shop' with stocks ranging from piles of bully beef, tinned milk and vegetables to marmalade and Wiltshire bacon, local chickens and even the odd cow. All this could be washed down with the local wine and crates of beer left in the cottage, and, if this was not enough, Major Angus McCorquodale, commanding Langley's company, had somehow managed to acquire a bottle of whisky and two bottles of sherry.

Major Angus McCorquodale

The next couple of days passed by with the heavy flow of traffic going through their front becoming a mere trickle. The only noteworthy event was the attempted shooting down of a low-flying plane. Brigadier Beckwith-Smith had earlier instructed the men on how to shoot an enemy aircraft down from the ground with the words:

> *'Stand up to them. Shoot at them with a Bren gun from the shoulder. Take them like a high pheasant. Give them plenty of lead. Remember, five pounds to any man who brings one down. I have already paid out ten pounds.'*

Fortunately, 'Becky' did not have to reach for his wallet, as the plane that passed by through the hail of bullets was later confirmed to be a British Lysander carrying Lord Gort who was having a last look at the perimeter defences of the BEF.

Sunday, 1 June started badly for Langley. One of his section commanders had got to grips with the rum ration rendering him useless, whilst a lone shell had hit a nearby barn, killing two of his men. A further surprise occurred when, as the thick early morning mist gave way to the rising sun, Langley observed to his amazement a group of some hundred Germans about 600 yards away in a field of green corn. Without hesitation, he ordered his Bren gunners to fire into them, which they did for a couple of minutes until nothing moved. A little while later some civilians, mostly women and children, were seen being herded by the odd German soldier towards their fallen comrades. The enemy rightly believed that the British soldiers would not fire on innocent French citizens, but they had not counted on accurate rifle fire, which killed three of them as they accompanied the innocent crowd.

Captain Evan Gibbs

Soon after this rather bizarre incident fighting began on all sections of the Coldstream front with shells raining down on their positions. At midday the Germans concentrated their attack on the right flank and No.1 Company, commanded by Captain Evan Gibbs, became hard-pressed, notably around the bridge they covered, which earlier that morning had been blown. No.3 Company's well-positioned guns helped ease their problems but were not enough to prevent the position from becoming virtually untenable. The Captain commanding the company of 5/Borders on Gibbs's right, informed Major McCorquodale that the Germans were massing for a further assault on the bridgehead and argued that they should prepare to withdraw while it was still possible to do so.

McCorquodale, however, realizing the importance of preventing a terminal breach to the defences, replied that such an action was out of the question: *'I order you to stay put and fight.'* When the Captain protested, McCorquodale told him that his men would shoot anyone seen retreating. A few minutes later the Captain was spotted making his way from the scene of the battle but a few shots from McCorquodale's rifle persuaded him otherwise.

There were, however, some lighter moments amid the growing struggle to hold the front. Indeed, during a lull in the fighting Bob Combe and Pop Wyatt, commanding No 2 Company on Langley's and McCorquodale's left, appeared, 'to see if they were all right.' It seems the real purpose of their mission was to have a strong drink, which McCorquodale duly

Captain Robert Combe

Major Pop Wyatt

A guardsman in action

offered them. *'Sherry? Whisky if you prefer it though I think we ought to save that as we may need it later.'* At that point he raised his glass, *'To a very gallant and competent enemy.'* By the end of the day only Langley among them would still be alive. Angus McCorquodale, who shunned the new British standard battledress, had declared earlier, *'I don't mind dying for my country but I'm not going to die dressed like a third-rate chauffeur.'* He got his wish and his passive body was easily recognizable, gleaming with polished brass and leather, as he lay in a field beside the cottage in which he had had his last drink.

Soon after this interval the battle had recommenced and once more much of it was heaped onto Evan Gibbs' Company. At one point one of his Bren guns was unmanned and Gibbs, who was worried the Germans might capture it, decided to attempt to recover the weapon himself, despite efforts to restrain him. He did not get very far before he was shot and, though a Guardsman very bravely ran out and carried him back, he died soon afterwards. This left the Company with one officer, Ronnie Speed, who had only just joined the Regiment. McCorquodale still insisted that the company should not withdraw and sent Langley with a flask full of liquor to give to Speed. Langley recalls:

> *'Ronnie was looking miserable, standing in a ditch up to his waist in water and shivering. I offered him Angus's flask and advised him to drink it, which he did. "You are not to retire. Do you understand?" He nodded, but was killed half an hour later when the enemy attacked and drove what was left of No 1 Company back onto us.'*

The battle raged on. A number of Bren gun firing pins melted away. Langley's cottage, which had already been singled out by incendiary anti-tank shells, was further victimized but amazingly never set on fire. Langley himself was sniping vigorously until injured by a shell bursting on the roof. He was carried out of the building and taken away from the fighting on a wheelbarrow. Fighting continued throughout the rest of the afternoon and casualties mounted, but the front was never broken. With the knowledge that they had held their defences as ordered, the Battalion withdrew at the appointed time of 10 o'clock under the cover of darkness. Fortunately the Germans, who were by this stage as exhausted as the withdrawing British defenders, did not press home their attack as the front thinned out. The action had cost many lives and the regiment, already depleted before the battle, was further decimated as a result of its vital and heroic defence of the canal.

What to see

The Bergues-Furnes canal is not a picturesque waterway, lined with shady trees and pretty buildings. Indeed, it is little more than a large wide ditch cutting through flat open countryside with the road from Bergues to Furnes on its south side. There are no obvious traces to be seen of the gallant defence by the East Lancashires, Coldstream Guards and other British battalions. However, from the records of the battle we can identify the area that Captain Ervine-Andrews and his B Company occupied. Shortly after leaving the village of Hoymille, there is a bridge across the canal signposted to Hameaux des Neiges. Continue past this and look out for tributary joining the main canal from the north. Records indicate that B Company of the East Lancs occupied the land just east of this. Ervine-Andrews' barn no longer exists and, not surprisingly, with a number of houses being demolished and others erected, it is very difficult to identify precise locations.

The Coldstream defences began at the next bridge you reach and continued as far as the junction with the D79. There were numerous cottages and small farms for the defenders to chose from but to be absolutely certain which was Langley's is less easy. None today precisely match the description, but this is not surprising, given the passage of time, not to mention the damage that these buildings incurred in May/June 1940. Visitors will want to walk part of the canal and see for themselves the open nature of the countryside, which gave the defenders such good fields of view and fire. How very different this exposed, rather gloomy area is from the solid fortress of Bergues!

FURNES

The defence of Furnes/Veurne, on the eastern edge of the Allied perimeter, was imperative. If it fell then it would be only a matter of hours before the Germans would reach the vital embarkation beaches at De Panne and seriously disrupt the evacuation.

The town is in Belgium but there are no customs or passport controls to worry about as you cross the border. Indeed, you could easily be forgiven for missing the fact that you had left France. The town is best reached by taking the toll-free coastal motorway – the E40 – until you reach Junction 1. Here you will see signs for 'Veurne' and, after less than a mile on the N8, the signs for the town centre become clearly marked on the right. My advice is to park in the Grote Markt, which is the main

St Walpurga's Church.

German soldiers on the move. British troops arrived in the town at the same time as the enemy.

square. Driving around Furnes is tricky with many confusing one-way streets, which seem designed to thwart the visitor.

Like so many towns in Belgium, Furnes endured heavy bombardments in 1940 and its recovery is particularly impressive. Amazingly, some buildings in the market square survived the German onslaught, while others have been carefully restored to their original 17th Century renaissance style. Today Furnes' bustling market town atmosphere is a far cry from the terror and noise caused by incessant sniper fire and artillery bombardments that were an endemic part of life here during its desperate defence in late May 1940.

1st and 2nd Battalions of the Grenadiers Guards were in no doubt that the defence of Furnes was going to be their biggest test yet. It was a key point in the eastern half of the perimeter and their orders were to hold it until told otherwise. News that the two East Surrey battalions were grimly defending the coastal town of Nieuport, several miles east of Furnes, was hardly encouraging, nor were the continuous salvo of shells that whipped in among them as they neared the end of their fifteen-mile route march. Most alarming of all was the sight of the Germans making their way towards the town, as Signalman George Jones of 1/Grenadiers remembers:

'At one stage on this same march, Harry came up alongside and with a backward jerk of his head drew my attention over to our right rear. About a mile away and out of range as far as we were concerned, a party of Germans could be seen marching and wheeling bicycles at about the same speed as our own column. Friend and foe arrived in Furnes at about the same time.

We took up positions on one side of the canal and most of the Germans the other.'

It soon became clear that movement around the solid brick red town, bisected by a fly-haunted canal, full of sunken barges, was extremely hazardous. Although the Germans were situated on the eastern side, a number of them had managed to take up sniper positions in the Allied half. Nevertheless, a reconnaissance of the area was vital and Lieutenant Colonel Jack Lloyd, the Commanding Officer of the 2nd Battalion, along with two of his company commanders, prepared to pace out the poplar-shaded towpath that was their sector of the canal (2/Grenadiers held the central part of the town and the 1st Battalion its southern outskirts). As they set off, a passing sapper sergeant urged, *'Don't go any further. There are snipers.'* After an uneventful five minutes, Lieutenant Colonel Lloyd decided to press on with the task of allotting company sectors. Suddenly three shots rang out and the three officers fell.

Acting on the spur of the moment, Second Lieutenant Jack Jones, who had watched the incident with horror, rushed out to their aid. Under heavy rifle and machine-gun fire, he carried the Commanding Officer, who was already dead, and then the two Company Commanders, Major Pakenham and Captain Jeffreys, into a nearby house. Such was the firepower directed on the building that it proved impossible for stretcher-bearers to approach it. Jones, assisted by a couple of other officers, did, however, manage to make an entrance through the back of the house and extricate them. Sadly

The section of the towpath where Lieutenant Colonel Lloyd and two Company Commanders fell victim to sniper fire.

the two Company Commanders died soon after and they, along with Lloyd, were later buried in the Close of St Walpurga's Church.

There was little time to reflect on this triple tragedy but the Battalion was undoubtedly rocked by such an event. Sergeant H.J. Mitchell remembers the reaction of the men around him:

'Throughout the Battalion there appeared a great sense of shock, but at the same time there was also a feeling of anger that reacted badly for the Germans when they came in to attack.'

The Battalion War Diary also records anger at the lack of professionalism of the troops they were sent in to relieve:

'The occupation of the town and the loss of life to the Battalion and to the 2nd Battalion Middlesex Regiment, who had supported us into position, might have been avoided if the British troops and French soldiers holding the town on the previous day had not been drunk when we entered it.'

Major Richard Colvin took over the Battalion and, before long, dispositions were allotted along the canal. Battalion Headquarters was established in a cellar in the main square, which had, according to the War Diary, been occupied by a fifth columnist who was 'discovered and executed.'

Shells were pouring down on the town, and the house above the Headquarters was soon reduced to rubble, as were many of the buildings around the centre. All around Furnes, houses were ablaze and thick acrid smoke filled the air. Under appalling difficulties the Grenadiers managed to occupy the houses overlooking the canal. Many, however, were forced by the terrific bombardment to seek refuge in the cellars. It was a town full of tension with streets and alleys alive with sharpshooters and Germans creeping through the ruins. Movement around the town was forbidden except for stretcher-bearers, signalmen and those fetching rations for the troops barricaded in the houses. Nowhere was safe, even as far back as Brigade Headquarters where vital conferences were held in a slit trench dug through the middle of a manure heap, with a straw and dung roof for camouflage. If the shells did not distract the commanders then the stench and insects certainly did.

To make matters worse, the Grenadiers were also desperately short of ammunition and the fifty guns of the 2/Middlesex supporting them were down to six rounds a day. Furthermore, defences to the north and south of the town were terribly thin. Harry Dennis, a driver in the 1/East Surreys, had discovered this a day earlier when he had been given a message to the Commanding Officer of the Berkshire Regiment ordering them to man the line just north of Furnes, next to the 2/Grenadiers:

'I eventually found them. They looked as though they had been put through a mincer. I approached a young officer. "I'm looking for the Commanding Officer of the Berkshires," I said. "That's me," he replied. He was a Lieutenant, not a Colonel or Major or Captain. It appeared they were

down to 87 men in the Battalion!'

It transpired that the Berkshires had got misdirected and come across a corner of the line where the Germans intercepted them. Despite their ordeal they willingly formed up on the perimeter. Dennis found their attitude in stark contrast to the resignation of some of his fellow Allied soldiers:

'5,000 Belgian soldiers came through our line, all on bikes. They moved into a nunnery near Furnes and my Colonel went in to make enquiries, as we desperately needed as many fighting men as possible. "What's all this about – why can't you come out and get on the line out there?" They replied that they had already been given their orders to stand down. We couldn't understand their capitulation. After all, there were 5,000 blokes sitting on their bums and our blokes out there were really struggling to hold the line.'

It was not only the Belgians who were unwilling to join the line. While many Frenchmen were heroically defending the western edge of the perimeter, the same cannot be said of some of their compatriots on the eastern side. Allan Younger of the Royal Engineers remembered one

Belgian troops were beginning to lose their will to carry on fighting as news of their nation's capitulation became known.

unsavoury incident along the Furnes Canal:

'I remember there was a French officer who had made some defences along the bank of the canal line with some French troops. He kept shouting at any French soldiers passing by "Remember Verdun. We must stand here. We mustn't let the Boches take Dunkirk." A quarter of a mile on, I heard a rifle shot and turned back to be told by one of the British soldiers behind us that a Frenchman had just shot this officer.'

Despite the Furnes defences being bolstered by the presence of 1/Coldstream, which was placed in reserve on the outskirts, the odds of holding the front were long. With the German 56th Division marching towards the town it seemed only a matter of time before it would fall. The Germans certainly thought so and Captain Neugart of the 25th Bicycle Squadron, which was already at Furnes, sent a captured French major into the town to demand a surrender from the British defenders. He received a scornful reply.

By midnight on 30 May countless attempts by the enemy to cross the canal using rubber boats had failed. These dinghies proved no match against rifle fire and were easily sunk. More problematic by far was the murderous shellfire that continued to burst all around their defences. Signalman Jones recalls:

'We saw and felt the town of Furnes tumble about us. The Germans expended untold quantities of ammunition upon the area, and us! Driven into the depths of cellars, rows of red bricked houses became an inferno of

Numerous German attempts to cross the canal were thwarted.

exploding rooftops.'

The Grenadiers also had to deal with the snipers that were all about the town. Major Colvin sent out numerous parties to hunt them down and all remaining civilians were herded into the crypt of the Church of St Walpurga on the Grand Place to make their job easier. Yet their efforts proved futile and Sergeant Mitchell recalls that not even the cellar was safe:

'Suddenly a shot rang out in the darkness, then a great CLANG as a bullet ricocheted off the ceiling girder and hit the steel helmet worn by Guardsman Lakin. Luckily, no injury was caused, but the language was a bit hot.'

Only the brave or the foolish risked movement around the town. The former applied to the Reverend Philip Wheeler, Padre to the Coldstream Guards, who gave communion to the troops in the cellars, ditches and trenches of the front line.

At 1 o'clock on 31 May the Garrison faced its most dangerous threat yet. The left flank defences of the town, manned by the depleted Berkshires and Suffolks, began collapsing as a result of repeated enemy assaults. The Coldstream reserves stabilized the situation by launching a costly but ultimately successful counter-attack which left at least forty officers and men either dead or badly wounded. Before long the Germans attacked again, to exploit this weakness in the Furnes defences. After some vicious fighting, around twenty German soldiers managed to cross the canal, where they sniped vigorously until a brave Lance Corporal led a section attack which killed off all of them at the cost of only one slight casualty.

Nevertheless the front was by now clinging on by a knife-edge and not surprisingly morale, particularly among the troops on the Grenadiers' left, was deteriorating fast. This was confirmed when a distraught sapper rushed into 2/Grenadiers Headquarters and informed Colvin that the left flank had once again been broken and that the Germans were coming across unopposed. He recalled:

'Second Lieutenant Jones was sent to investigate and found that the remnants of the Berkshires and Suffolk, along with soldiers from 246 Field Company Royal Engineers, were about to withdraw. Jones attempted to reorganize and rally them, but when some broke under further heavy shellfire he found it necessary to shoot some of the men, and his NCOs turned others at the point of the bayonet. Jones then organized and led a counter-attack, which not only resulted in the re-establishment of positions along the bank but which also seems to have restored the men's morale.'

His Military Cross citation reads:

'By his prompt and determined action and his leadership regardless of enemy fire, he undoubtedly saved a situation which would otherwise have had disastrous results. His coolness and conduct was an inspiring example to all.'

German artillerymen bring a 10.5cm piece into position to lay down fire on British and French positions.

By early evening the German assaults ebbed away, to be replaced by even heavier shell bombardments. Indeed these had become so serious that the men had little option but to hide in the cellars and just hope they lived through it. The Flemish town was suffering cruelly. Most of the 17th century buildings ringing the market place were reduced to heaps of rubble and the churchyard of St Walpurga was said to be so thick with shrapnel that it was like trampling over a carpet of jagged glass. Another Jones, Signalman George Jones, sheltered in one of the cellars at the Grand Place:

> *'Now pinned down, movement outside became impossible but at least the same could be said for the enemy and, since our precise cellar remained impervious to shot and shell, we had little option but to sit back in comparative safety to rest, wait and hope for the best. Someone scrounging around found a portable wireless and at around 2.00pm we heard the news that, "Over two-thirds of the forces encircled in the area of Dunkirk have now been evacuated and are safely in England." In the gloom of dark corners of the cellar, looks and silence betrayed the thoughts of every one of us. Here we were miles inland and virtually trapped in a town collapsing from bombardments from both sides. Meanwhile the best part of the Army was safely back in England. It felt very lonely.'*

Little did he know that an hour later an order would be received telling the entire garrison to withdraw. Most of the troops were to leave at 10.00pm while a few would have to hold the line until 2.00am. Everyone knew that it would be a difficult and dangerous operation, but it was their only hope. Nevertheless, for Jones and the departing troops running the fiery gauntlet of the intense shelling, it was a terrifying prospect. Then, as they made their way out of the cellars, all of a sudden the bombardment ceased. He remembers:

> *'For us, our first miracle of Dunkirk then began. This curtain of ragged steel began to lift just before 10.00pm and, in the bright red glow of a hundred fires, we walked from Furnes without a bomb, shell or bullet arriving within half a mile of our scrambling single files. Twice we took wrong turnings almost walking down the throat of the enemy but, stumbling over piles of rubble, bricks, broken glass and tangled telephone wires, at last we were clear. Having not volunteered to stay behind until 2.00pm, I had a sense of deep respect towards those we had left behind us and much later when able, I voiced my appreciation and feelings to one of my mates who remained to man the skeleton command post. With typical generosity he answered, "Guts my foot, Wacky. I was too bloody scared to leave that cellar!" I never believed him.'*

Silently the Grenadiers began moving out. All knew that any sound might reveal their intention to the enemy, but keeping quiet was easier said than done as they contended in the darkness with the debris of battle. Sergeant Mitchell's platoon was ordered to move out first and cover a vital road junction ahead.

> *'When we arrived at the junction all was quiet and we set up positions covering the roads from Furnes and Nieuport. Sergeant Hirst and I were responsible for the Furnes Road and Sergeants Reed and Noble the Nieuport Road. Our own Battalion started coming through about 2.00am and by 4.00am it was mainly stragglers. Then, as if the Germans had woken up to the fact that Furnes was quiet, we were treated to shelling which was very accurate on the area. Guardsman Baines and one other were wounded and one of our carriers knocked out. Some people on the Nieuport road were also caught and we could hear the wounded crying out. Stan Hirst and I were on the Brens when we heard the noise of horses galloping towards us from Furnes. What was it? Cavalry? Germans driving the horses as cover? We quickly got behind the hedge and at least 40 horses completely filling the road raced past, but no Germans followed. It was a very scary moment and worse than the shells.'*

By 2.30am the last of the British defenders were moving out of Furnes and the surrounding area towards the beaches and, for the lucky ones, evacuation.

What to see

The Grote Markt, formerly the Grande Place, has a helpful Tourist Information Centre that will provide a map of the area. It was around here, with fires raging all around and with endless bombardments shattering above them, that many British troops, like Signalman George Jones, hid in cellars. It is worth visiting the Church of St Walpurga, which is easily recognizable just beyond the Tourist Information Centre. It was in the pleasant park surrounding the Church that Lieutenant Colonel Jack Lloyd and his two Company Commanders were initially buried, having been shot by sniper fire. Their bodies now rest in Furnes Cemetery.

The canal, dissecting the town, is full of activity and it is well worth strolling along its banks and shaded towpath. Your walk will be an altogether more peaceful one than that fateful reconnaissance by Lieutenant Colonel Lloyd and the two Company Commanders. In 1940 the canal was full of sunken barges and its width was undoubtedly a formidable obstacle to the attackers.

Make your way either on foot or, if you brave it, by vehicle to the Furnes Cemetery on the north east of the town centre, along Oude Vestingstrate. The Commonwealth War Graves are on the left as you enter. In the furthest corner is Lieutenant Colonel Lloyd's final resting place. A total of seventy-nine officers and men are buried here: seventy-two soldiers and seven airmen. As well as Grenadiers and Coldstreamers, Black Watch, Green Howards, The Northumberland Regiment, The Loyals, Royal Artillery and RAMC are represented. Evidence of the intense shelling and bombing at Furnes is apparent from the number of civilians killed over the period of May-June 1940.

The Grote Markt, with the tower of St Nicholas' Church in the background. After the war, many of the old buildings were restored and it is now hard to believe that the town was the scene of such destruction in 1940.

Chapter Five

THE BEACHES

De Panne/La Panne can be reached from Dunkirk either by taking the main coastal motorway, the E40, turning off at Junction 1a or alternatively by using the D940/N1. If approaching from Furnes, take the N8. La Panne is a thriving Belgian seaside town, which has undergone much change since 1940. It is the country's premier holiday resort and has a modern but generally tasteful feel, despite the extensive building that has recently taken place. The town could, however, be in danger of being overrun by high-rise apartments. Apart from the beach itself, La Panne bears little resemblance to the place that brought salvation to thousands of battle-weary BEF troops and the noise of Stukas has been replaced by the sound of cement mixers in their seemingly never-ending quest to maximize any space available. Nevertheless, it is well worth wandering around the town and beach, and you will certainly find no shortage of cafés, restaurants and hotels, should you need them.

Bray Dunes was another vital embarkation location. From La Panne take the coastal road west for some seven kilometres and you will see the town clearly marked. As you approach the town, it is worth stopping the car and climbing to a vantage point. Rather than seeing a beach, there are dunes stretching for miles to the east, west and north. This must have been a wearying sight for members of the BEF, tired, hungry and sorely harried by the Germans. In stark contrast to the tourist ambitions of La Panne, it is a sprawling and slightly colourless seaside town, which has seen little change since the war years.

Bray Dunes has changed little over the the years. A visit there will leave you in no doubt as to why it is so named.

A ship's launch tows lifeboats crowded with men – too laborious, too slow.

The Early days of Embarkation

The beaches along the coast shelve very gradually and presented the Navy with a very real problem as their destroyers and other large vessels were often unable to get closer than a mile from them. Contrary to popular myth, there were no small civilian crafts to pick up the hordes of troops during the first few days. The ships were therefore forced to use their own small landing crafts to ferry the men out. Such a process was desperately

A view from a steamer. This well-known photograph clearly shows the lack of organization that marked the early days of the evacuation.

slow. Indeed, by the evening of 27 May Lord Gort and his headquarters estimated that no more than 200 men had been lifted off the beaches. It transpires that the number was more like 2,500, but the fact remains that the process was alarmingly time-consuming. Furthermore, after a massive Luftwaffe raid on the port earlier that day, it was agreed that Dunkirk harbour could not be used for evacuation. This meant that the beaches stretching from Dunkirk to La Panne were the only hope for the Allied forces.

The poor results of this first day seemed to confirm many people's fears that the task of evacuating the entire BEF was an impossible one. Churchill believed that 10,000 troops could be lifted every twenty-four hours. Even this would be nowhere near enough, as most envisaged that Dunkirk would fall within two or three days, but it now seemed he had been over optimistic. Major James Moulton and others working in Gort's Headquarters attempted to ignore such negative thoughts:

> *'Estimation of how many men we could get out per day would have been too gloomy altogether. At GHQ level we were so used to seeing arrows on our maps which showed the German tanks were right behind us that it was better not to think of what might happen tomorrow.'*

Optimism or no optimism, one thing was certain – the rate of embarkation had to be quickened. The main problem was that the naval boat crews were not used to this ferrying work and soon exhaustion, from rowing to and from their ships, was affecting them as much as it was the battle-weary troops.

To add to their woes, once the sailors reached the shore they were confronted by desperate soldiers who had little idea as to how to embark. Many boats were turned over as the troops tried to clamber into them. Few were aware that the vessels had to be head to sea before being boarded. The task of manoeuvring them around whilst they were laden with men could and did result in either grounding, swamping or, worse still, capsizing. Vic Chanter was part of a Royal Navy landing party and initially found the loading extremely tricky:

> *'Some of the boats became overloaded, sticking into the sand. At this point, it proved virtually impossible to persuade the troops to jump out in order to lighten the load, though we tried to assure them that we would allow them back in once we could reach deeper water.'*

Obviously the landing parties could not be expected to row back and forth to the ships for ever, and troops were given the task under naval supervision. However, Chanter, like many, soon encountered further hazards when combining soldiers with sea-faring vessels:

> *'On one such occasion, three of us (RN) had just managed to refloat a full to the gunwales cutter. "Okay, row like hell! Get going," we screamed at them. All of a sudden I felt and heard an almighty bang; I'd been hit on*

the back of the head and fell forward into the sea. Some time later the situation became clear and, on reflection, a bit of a laugh. The soldiers in the boat had responded incredibly well to the order to "Get going", but on one side only. Consequently the cutter swung round ninety degrees, got caught up in the swell and came down on me. I guess the lads on the boat got home somehow.'

It was not only the rowing boats that struggled in such adverse circumstances. The few available motor launches also had difficulties, largely because of debris in the water. All too often clothes, equipment, corpses and ropes were caught up in the propellers, thereby rendering them useless. They too were often swamped through massive overcrowding. Sailors recognized that only firm action could stave off further tragedy and strict discipline whilst boarding was soon demanded. Men's fingers were clubbed off the gunwales by sailors desperate to save their boat and sometimes, as Major Robert Tong, an officer at GHQ, witnessed, the use of revolvers was deemed necessary:

'One ship's officer was trying to keep the boat from broaching to, because the swell was pushing it around. The people getting on board were adding to the problem by pulling on the boat. The captain told them to let go but was threatened with the butt end of a rifle. At this point, the naval officer pulled out a pistol aimed and yelled, "Look you, let go or else". The soldier in question duly obliged.'

The truth is that discipline among the first troops attempting to embark almost entirely broke down. Leaderless, lost and confused, swarms of men roamed the dunes, some drunk, some weaponless and nearly all thoroughly dispirited, as the bombs rained down around them. Most had been separated from their units over the past days and weeks of fighting by accident, indiscipline or cowardice. Order gave way to self-preservation, and the scenes that followed were far from savoury. A report written after the event cited that some ambulance men abandoned their much-needed vehicles; a number of military policemen neglected their duties and many officers simply deserted their troops. It was every man for himself and rushes for the limited boats were the inevitable consequence.

The troops in the water were, however, under extreme pressure, and it was hard to keep calm when some small vessel, capable of holding perhaps ten men, finally came within reach. Jostling for positions ensued as the men raced to meet it. Charles Nash observed that a considerable number lost their lives as a result of terror and indiscipline:

'An equal number of casualties were caused by panic in the form of people falling over and drowning, and lifeboats capsizing as they tried to scramble into them, as were caused by Luftwaffe activity.'

For many, like Nash who spent six days on the beaches and in the water, it was a long frustrating wait for the trickle of boats that made their way to

Orderly queues quickened the rate of embarkation, but did not lessen the dangers. Many drowned as they waded out to waiting vessels.

the shore.

> *'Often we'd get so near to one of these boats, when Jerry would come down and start strafing. At this point, it was just a gigantic dispersal exercise. Waiting for those boats was soul-destroying.'*

In fact, the majority of troops did not get lifted off by the small naval cutters but were forced to wade a long way out to sea to reach larger vessels waiting some hundreds of metres away from the beach. Lines of men, often up to their necks in water, waited expectantly for boats to come to their rescue. This was extremely hazardous because as the tide rose, so the risk to men at the front increased. Soldiers were reluctant to give up their place, return to the back of the queue and face the further wrath of divebombers. The gamble to stay was often a fatal one. Alfred Cromwell, serving aboard HMS *Kellet*, remembers the danger of waiting in the sea:

> *'The boat crews said they saw a lot of men drowned by pressure from the back as the men waded out – it doesn't take a lot for you to be pushed out of your depth.'*

Sometimes those at the end of the queues were ordered to swim out to the waiting boats. Captain Bill Burbridge recalls:

> *'Someone shouted, "There's your boat and you have to try and get to it. It wasn't long before we were out of our depth and had to swim for it. I am afraid that quite a number didn't make it.'*

Even when troops did reach the ships it was not always easy getting on board. Oliver Anderson, a Chief Petty Officer on HMS *Sutton*, had particular difficulties with an overweight Major:

> *'He must have been all of sixteen stone. We had scrambling nets but he couldn't make it up them. In the end we threw him a heaving line, which he tied round his waist in a slipknot. Everybody on board was desperately heaving. Eventually he made it but not until after we had nearly cut him in two.'*

By the end of 28 May the rate of embarkation was increasing, but it was still desperately slow. HMS *Malcolm's* record at La Panne reflected the poor performance on all the beaches in the first few days. In fifteen hours the destroyer had managed to pick up only 450 men. The hopelessness of the situation was plain to see for the increasing numbers of troops arriving on the beaches. Lance Bombardier Cyril Beard, a surveyor in the Royal Artillery, was one of these men:

'We arrived at the top of the dunes to be presented with an extraordinary sight. The dunes were plastered with troops. On the beach were two columns which formed to feed two small boats which were being rowed to and from to a vessel of some 3000 tonnes.'

Back at his Headquarters cut in the Dover cliffs, Admiral Ramsay, who was made aware of the embarkation problems by HMS *Wakeful's* succinct radio message 'Plenty troops, few boats', worked hard to rectify the problem. While only 6,000 men were lifted on 28 May, every day would see a substantial rise in the number rescued to the point where three days later that figure would be quadrupled.

One reason for the improving numbers being lifted was that incidents of disorder were now becoming rare. The work of Captain E.G. Tennant, RN, twelve officers and 160 ratings sent over by Ramsay the day before to take control of the evacuation, was beginning to pay off. Beachmasters, allocated by Tennant to the various embarkation points, restricted the numbers of troops waiting on the beaches. It was not too long before orderly zig-zag queues, three men abreast, could be seen stretching into the sea. George Viner was the beachmaster at La Panne for four days:

Captain E G Tennant

'Nobody was allowed on the beaches unless he had a pass, allocated at HQ. As men got off the beach so I would call for more men to come down. It was a steady trickle, but we didn't present ourselves as a feasible bombing target.'

Some, like Sergeant Ken Naylor, having witnessed the carnage that Stuka divebombers caused amongst the queues, disagreed. They were reluctant to join the 'suicidal' lines and sought their own means of reaching ships off shore.

'Once more we were treated to a raid by the Luftwaffe and once again were very lucky; they seemed to be aiming at the troops standing in the water. We carried on down the beach, disregarding the orders of several officers who wanted us to join the "queue in the sea". Our remarks were unprintable after seeing what happened to some of the men standing in the water! Ten or more minutes later we were rewarded with a marvellous sight, a ship's lifeboat upside down at the water's edge. I inspected the upturned boat, found that there were no holes or cracks and that the bung, a large brass one which screwed into the bottom was intact... The boat was pushed out into

Queuing soldiers posed an easy target for Luftwaffe pilots.

about 3-4 feet of water and everyone put in place. The oars were placed in the water and I gave the command "give way all" to the rowing rhythm of "IN-OUT, IN-OUT" and we were under way, straight for a destroyer some three-quarters of a mile out.'

Naylor and his men were certainly not alone in trying to find their own means of embarkation. A number of soldiers ignored the beachmasters in their service dress and with red bands on their arms, who had been sent over from the UK, and discipline was often only restored with the use of their revolvers. Leonard Howard found himself on the receiving end of one such incident:

'Two chaps were paddling out in a flimsy canoe when a Stuka came down and machine-gunned them. They both drowned and the boat drifted upside down some way off the beach. I knew Sergeant Baldry could swim well and thought there was a chance of getting it. At that moment, one of the beachmasters yelled out, "Come out of the water!" We were damned if we were going to follow his instructions until he fired a couple of shots from his revolver which slipped into the water bloody close to us.'

Tempers were tested and the language was ripe as soldiers waited in line. In such desperate hours, rank was not always adhered to as Captain Stanley Hill remembers when helping embark one infantry brigade:

'The old brigade commander, a splendid old boy with grey hair, got on this lifeboat with a number of his men. They were, however, too heavy and so he said, "Come on boys, get off, we'll give her a shove". So he jumped off along with a few other soldiers and they gave the boat a push. Away the

lifeboat went without him, with all the men waving goodbye. I've never seen a Brigadier so angry in my life.'

The reactions of the troops throughout this terrifying time were varied. There were examples of tremendous selflessness. Eric Knight, serving with the Royal Ambulance Medical Corps, was particularly touched by one such act:

> *'A small boat was leaving the beach and loaded to the gunwales with troops. An officer in the boat saw me carrying a stretcher. "What have you got there?" he shouted. "Been badly wounded, I'm afraid Sir," I replied. He stopped the boat and said, "Right, who's coming out?" Four men who had probably been waiting for days got out straight away and gave their place to a wounded comrade. In doing so they had given up the answer to their prayers. The last I saw of them was going to the back of the queue.'*

For some, the pressure of waiting on the beaches, having already endured weeks of heavy fighting, was just too much. Leonard Howard witnessed a number of soldiers taking their own life:

> *'I saw at least half a dozen men commit suicide by running into the sea. They were under terrific strain. Some would just scream and shoot themselves.'*

Panic was not uncommon and soldiers were sometimes shot by men on their own side if this jeopardized the speed and safety of embarkations. Edgar Rabbets of 5/Northamptonshire Regiment was queuing up for embarkation on one of the small boats when an army officer in front of him

British troops at Bray Dunes await their turn to join the queues for ships. Some, under the constant attention of the Luftwaffe, had to endure up to four days on the beaches.

was shot for rushing:

'He was determined to get on one of these boats. It was obvious he'd had a rough time because he was trying to exert his authority, not only by his rank but also by waving his revolver around. After one or two efforts at restraining the man, one of his fellow officers shot him.'

While stories of heroism abound, there were also cases of cowardice. Sergeant-Major William Knight of the Royal Engineers was left with an uneasy feeling after watching an officer act in a far from gallant fashion:

'He was wildly brandishing his revolver and threatening these two Tommies who were trying to get into the boat. At this point he wasn't in it himself but, when it set off, he jumped onto it himself and left the two frightened soldiers in the water.'

Not everybody was eager to wade into the sea to meet the boats that promised their salvation. A number of troops could not swim and some, like 20-year-old Private Sidney Barley of the King's Own Scottish Borders, were terrified of water. His sister, Alice Jacklin, tells the story:

'Mum later got a telegram "missing presumed killed", but she never believed he was dead right up to the day that she died. Dad and I knew he could not be alive because if he had to go out into the sea he wouldn't be able to do it. When he was young, a boy at school pushed him in the deep end of the swimming baths and after that he was terrified of water. One of the lads (only seven soldiers came home from the whole of his regiment) later came to see mum and he said my brother was the life and soul of the Battalion. The last he saw of him was on the beach. He heard him say to another chap, "I'm going back to Lille. I'm not going in the water. So long, chum".'

Where possible, Army chaplains provided spiritual comfort amidst the horror. A number of makeshift altars were erected along the beaches where men received Holy Communion, prayed and sang hymns. The calm leadership of the men leading these proceedings was much admired. Leonard Howard recalls:

'The padres were marvellous. We had a padre who stayed behind. He refused to be embarked because he'd decided his job was to stay with the prisoners.'

Lorry Jetties

The establishment of order among the troops and the increasing numbers of vessels arriving daily from Britain were certainly vital factors in the rising rates of embarkation. It was, however, the idea to build lorry jetties that provided the most ingenious improvement in the evacuation from the beaches. Anything that could aid the loading of men on to the small boats was to be welcomed, and these improvised piers did just that. The concept is widely believed to have originated at La Panne where a military policeman, Lieutenant Harold Dibbens, noted that some form of jetty stretching into the sea could dramatically reduce the clumsiness of the current procedure.[1]

Unlike most members of the retreating army, Dibbens was thoroughly at home on the sea, having been brought up on the Isle of Wight. It was clear to him that if a jetty was built then boats could come alongside and be loaded more efficiently. Not only would it counter the risk of capsizing and running aground, but it would also prevent boats from being turned the wrong way by troops, tide or wind.

This was all very well in theory, but how could a pier be built in so little time? The mass of abandoned lorries strewn around the quay side soon provided the answer. Under his own initiative, Dibbens got to work. Men of 102 Provost Company were ordered to bring the lorries on to the beach, where they were then driven out as far as possible at low tide. Here they were attached with cable to each other by a group of thirty Royal Engineers under the supervision of Captain E.H. Sykes. To counter the risk of the lorries drifting off, their tyres were burst. Sandbags and any other heavy objects nearby were loaded into them for further weight and stability. It was a race against time, as sappers had to secure the jetty while the tide was coming in around them. They laboured tirelessly, as did the 'Provosts', who proved themselves to be extremely proficient scavengers, providing not only the lorries, but also the wood for a plank walkway. By dawn on 30 May the 'Provost Jetty' was in use.

The improvised piers were not without their problems. A number were destroyed by the tide soon after completion. A poorly built jetty could sometimes be more of a hindrance than a help to sailors, who found that

Lorries were run out onto the beach and linked together to provide makeshift jetties.

some lorries spilt junk into the sea which was then caught up in the propellers of the boats. Soldiers also encountered difficulties as movement along the slippery wooden planks was extremely precarious. Overall, though, the effects of these lorry jetties were beneficial to the evacuation effort, as Vic Chanter explains:

> *'It was certainly a most welcome break for us. We of the RN Landing Party were thankful for these labour-saving piers, not least because no more brute force was required pushing the boats out and getting wet through.'*

Life on the Beaches

Lack of food was a major problem for the men as they waited on the beaches and dunes. A few soup stoves were set up, but the queues for these were almost as long as those stretching out to sea. Even when the men reached the end the quantity of soup they received, accompanied by stale bread and some tinned beef if lucky, did little to satisfy their appetites. Unfortunately but necessarily, many of the well-stocked lorries had been destroyed on entering the perimeter and soldiers were often forced to use their own initiative to prevent hunger from setting in. Looting was commonplace in the abandoned houses nearby and beaches were combed of any discarded rations that lay littered around. A few had success but the majority went hungry. Sometimes men were forced to take extreme measures and the sight of this in operation was a shocking reminder of the desperate plight of the Allied armies. Charles Nash could hardly believe his eyes at the reaction of a bunch of Belgian soldiers to a horse appearing on the beach:

> *'Immediately they made a mad rush to get it. Once the horse had been caught, they killed it and all those who could get anything out of it took it.'*

At one point during the evacuation a group of French nuns, ignoring the murderous machine gunning and bombing, attempted to relieve the suffering of these undernourished troops. Thomas Gunn witnessed their courage:

> *'The night before I got away, a handful of them came on the beaches and gave some coffee and rolls to as many of us as they could with no thought for themselves.'*

Some time before the actual evacuation was ordered the Navy had the foresight to disperse eighty thousand tons of fresh water along the beaches east of Dunkirk. This contingency measure eased initial problems of dehydration but it soon became clear that more was needed. Local water supplies had been damaged by the bombing and thirst became a major issue for the men as they waited in the sands. Some had little option but to leave the beaches and search for refreshment inland. They soon discovered that the local cellars were more than just a refuge from bombing and shelling, they were also often well stocked with wine and the sight of drunken soldiers staggering around was not uncommon. To many it seemed that alcohol was more widely available than drinking water. Soldiers like the men in Ernest Harris's unit had to improvise as best they could:

'We only had a drop of water and so that didn't last long. We did however manage to find a store jar with some rum in it – Navy rum, which was like treacle. Because we had no water, we mixed it with seawater. It tasted vile but certainly kept us warm.'

Indeed, while the days were often hot, the nights got very cold, especially for the large numbers of men who had waded out in vain when it was light. Blankets were a rare luxury and it was left to soldiers to rummage through the discarded packs and equipment strewn along the beaches. Extra clothing was rarely hard to find on the beaches. Vic Chanter recalls:

'We were constantly getting wet through, but we were never short of a change of uniform. All over the beach was the pick of the army, discarded uniforms, photos, everything! Perhaps some lucky ones found time to grab the few most treasured possessions that they could cram into their battledress pockets, but for the most it was the time for survival – and leaving old memories behind. So sadly, at times, whilst looking for dry clothing to put on, searching through the discarded packs strewn among the sands, I would come upon family photographs, with wives and children looking out at me, a complete stranger! Indications of haste and urgency required that a soldier couldn't stop to salvage from his own belongings the few very personal articles that were his alone – and not issued to him. One hoped that the owners of these keepsakes would soon be united with the ones

Casualties beside a water bowser. Eighty thousand tons of fresh water had been placed on the beaches by the Royal Navy for the gathering troops.

French Destroyer *Bourrasque* sinking off the coast of Dunkirk after hitting a mine, her decks crowded with troops.

in the photographs but not all of them would make it to England.'

Throughout this time the Luftwaffe were rampant and their continuous attacks ensured there were many men for whom the sands would be their eternal resting place. Göring had confidently asserted that his force would make any Allied evacuation attempt an impossibility. *'Only fishing boats can get over now. Let's hope the Tommies are good swimmers,'* he had joked just prior to the first British ships arriving off the coast. Beneath the humour there was a vain determination to prove the Wehrmacht generals wrong, as a number had openly expressed doubts as to the validity of the Air Field Marshal's promise. The Allied troops, who made easy targets in their huddles and lines, had little option but to endure everything that the German Airforce could throw at them. William Cassel, serving aboard the minesweeper HMS *Gossamer*, watched the raids with horror:

'Suddenly without warning the German fighters came in low over the beaches, machine gunning the men on the ground. It was all over in five minutes and the scenes were terrible. The only way I can describe it is like a farmer cutting corn.'

The majority of soldiers, like Gunner Norman Hammond in the 51/Light Ack Ack Regiment, had witnessed serious fighting over the past few weeks. Nothing, however, could have prepared them for the sights left in the wake of these Luftwaffe raids, many of which still live with the veterans today:

'In the dunes we were waiting and wondering, strafed and bombed, with men killed and wounded all around. Three of us crouched down behind the

Junkers 87 dive bombers – the most hated and feared aircraft of them all.

other during one attack. The first man bought it with shrapnel through his side – I know because blood was splattered over us. In the same raid one of our officers had his foot blown off. He was carried off. His foot, still in his boot, lay in the sand. Gory details I know, but this is the sort of thing that one remembers.'

Every soldier present on the beaches during this time witnessed tragedy all around him. Young Clifford Homey was particularly affected by one raid:

Ready to duck into 'bolt holes' in the sand at first sight of the Luftwaffe.

'Then came the Stukas with their bombs and machine guns and wingwailers. Unfortunately no RAF! All hell and no salvation. This passed and I went to find Coley. I found him after about half an hour of searching. He was sitting upright in a small trench. I got in beside him and said to him, "You were glad you'd got that bloody shovel." Coley didn't answer. I went to shove him and as I touched him he fell to one side. He was dead. No marks or bullet holes and no blood. But he was dead. Panic. What do you do in this carnage? Dead and injured lying around. I spotted an officer with the RAMC chevrons and went to tell him my mate was dead with no marks. His reply, "It happens, soldier." He came and had a look at him and said, "I'll take his dog-tags. You bury him if you wish." I did so. What a tragedy. Poor Coley had only been married for six months. What a terrible shock. Not 21 years old, but dead. Where is the justice?'

It is hard to imagine the noise that was generated by the Luftwaffe around the beaches as they wreaked havoc on the defenceless troops. The sound of the enemy aircraft seems to be the most powerful memory for those who survived this terrifying ordeal. Stanley Allen recalls that Stukas were the most hated of all the Luftwaffe fighters because of the noise they made: *'It really was a hell of a scream.'* Indeed the Stuka or Junker JU87B, which had been such an essential component of blitzkrieg earlier that month, was now used to deadly effect on the beaches of Dunkirk. The dive-bombing attacks on the troops were carried out at a steep angle of eighty-five degrees to give it pinpoint accuracy. The spats over the wheels were fitted with air-activated sirens and it was these that produced the nightmarish scream that so many veterans remember.

It is hardly worth contemplating the effect that Luftwaffe bombs would have had if the beaches of La Panne and Bray Dunes had been pebbles. Fortunately, though, the powdery sand seems to have had a deadening effect on them. It did, however, have the drawback of making it difficult for the troops to dig holes deep enough to provide necessary cover from bullets and shrapnel. This added to the troops' insecurities, as Ernest Harris recalls:

'It was the same in all the dunes – with sand like the sand out of egg-timers and tufts of grass everywhere. You just had to keep as low as you could, and hope and pray you lived.'

Spades were a rare commodity. Troops had little choice but to dig the foxholes and slit trenches with their hands, rifles or whatever equipment seemed most appropriate. Yet even in the relative cover of these, there were unforeseen hazards. Walter Richardson, an NCO in the 21/Anti-tank Regiment, soon realized that it was a mistake to dig too enthusiastically:

'We constantly faced shelling and dive-bombing. It seemed like we were always getting in or out of our bloody slit trench. One chap managed to dig himself a little too deep in the sand. When a couple of bombs dropped very

near, his slit trench caved in and he was buried alive. I myself got buried but was dug out just in time. It was terrifying being down there, unable to move, with this sand on top of you.'

It is worth remembering that many of these troops had faced almost continuous shellfire and bombing since 10 May. A few now began to crack under the pressure of these frenzied enemy raids. Edgar Rabbets observed visible signs of shellshock among the troops he was queuing with:

'One man used to just stand still. As soon as the guns started he just couldn't move. He was just completely paralysed. Others were very quiet. Some started trembling and shaking, getting all nervous and upset.'

Gradually most troops got used to the assaults from the sky. After the first day or so a surprising degree of calm and order was observed, even in the course of an attack. Corporal Harry Dennis, 1/East Surreys, recalled a typical moment.

'The Luftwaffe would just go along the beach, strafing up and down. It was just a matter of dodging the bullets. Often the blokes just lay out in the open. If they didn't get hit, they were lucky, but many did... What was amazing was that we got very used to it. There was nobody running amuck – dashing here and there.'

Amidst such massacre, examples of heroism abounded. William Knight, an NCO in the Royal Engineers, recalls an ultimate act of camaraderie:

'One chap was carrying a wounded man over his shoulder when another attack arrived. I dived for cover and when I looked out, I noticed he'd been

Increasingly, troops found putting up some resistance, however futile, was preferable to lying down defenceless on the sand.

unable to find cover so he'd put his wounded companion on the ground and was lying spread-eagled over the top of him.'

The Army's usual drill in an air raid was to hit the ground and stay there until the threat had passed. The effectiveness of such a policy was questionable, because the shrieking screams of the Stukas and in particular their bombs gave the troops lying face down the impression that they were going to land on top of them. It was not long before fear turned to rage, and many defiantly started shooting at the Heinkels and Stukas as they tore along the beaches. Their rifles and Bren guns proved ineffective against the planes' armour-plated bellies, but the soldiers at least seemed to take some solace in this gesture of defiance.

If the men's predicament was unenviable, so too was the position of those German pilots forced to bale out anywhere near the beaches. Not surprisingly, they were given a less than friendly reception and soldiers found their rifles considerably more effective on the parachutists floating down than they did on the aircraft which had carried them. Such reactions were not savoury but were understandable given that the troops had not only endured continuous bombing, shelling and strafing, but had also witnessed the sinking of a number of loaded vessels. Douglas Smith was particularly upset by the deliberate sinking of clearly marked hospital ships:

'I remember watching the Queen of the Channel steaming towards Dunkirk. She was all painted with red and white crosses and everything. Looked glorious. I had been on her on a day trip to Calais several years before the war. All of a sudden, a bomber went over her and she blew up then and there and sank. It was ghastly seeing this lovely hospital ship go down like that, and I think it affected us all.'

Morale was also affected by the constant rumours that circulated around the troops. Reg Bazeley explains:

'A rumour circulated that a U-Boat had got into the fleet of boats out at sea, and this then seemed to be confirmed by a huge explosion. We later learnt it was HMS Wakeful. Our spirits were also tested by the German aircraft who dropped leaflets advising the men on the beaches to "give up because you have no RAF left, and all the Generals have gone home". The lads swore and they used the leaflets for earthier purposes! A story circulated that General Gort and his entourage had been called back to England leading to a lot of pessimism and such comments as "We will never get back" and "They have deserted us". These doubts were quite widespread. Another rumour arose that we were going to surrender and that we had already asked for terms. This was not true, of course, but at the time it seemed to have credence. Such rumours create panic.'

Fortunately, in the later stages, the firm discipline demanded of the men ensured that few showed visible manifestations of fear. They realized that they had little choice but to wait and hope for their return to Blighty.

Last days on the beaches

By 30 June time was running out. While the evacuation of troops was quickening with every hour, there seemed to be no let-up in the number of battle-weary troops who were making their way down the corridor and on to the dunes. One thing was clear to the men queuing on the beachfront – the pitch of the defensive actions seemed to be getting closer. Ernest Victor, and the men around him, were left with an increasingly uneasy feeling as doubts were now raised about whether they could be lifted off in time:

> *'We thought we were never going to get away. We didn't know what the devil was happening. No one seemed to know. There still seemed far too few boats lifting the boys off. Everyone was just sitting around in the dunes. We knew the rear guard were fighting at the back of us to stop the Germans coming through, because the din was terrible.'*

Some of the soldiers were becoming restless. No one needed reminding that the vessels that were lifting them off the beaches were the difference between years of captivity or freedom. By this stage the first of an armada of little boats were beginning to appear on the horizon. Many had shallow drafts, ideal for lifting off the beaches, and the numbers of men embarking continued to rise impressively.

Under constant threat from the Luftwaffe, these vessels, mostly manned by civilian volunteers, worked tirelessly ferrying men from the shores to the waiting ships further out. On 30 June alone some 29,000 men were rescued from the beaches. The evacuation, despite heavy losses of men and craft, was going better than anyone had dared expect. However, with the Germans closing in and a massive 180,000 Allied servicemen still in and

The Germans were closing in and breaking through the perimeter. Here a machine gun team cross one of the numerous water barriers. TAYLOR LIBRARY

around Dunkirk, there was little time to appreciate the success of the operation to date.

On 1 June it became clear that the perimeter defences were breaking. La Panne would soon fall into enemy hands and an order came through that the eastern end of the beaches was to be abandoned. The only course of action was to march the bulk of the troops down the beach towards Dunkirk. Inevitably the numbers lifted off the beaches fell as the troops pulled back from La Panne. The harbour, and in particular the mole, which was already proving invaluable to the Allied escape now became vital.

It is worth sparing a thought for those exhausted soldiers who, having arrived at La Panne after their desperate defence of the perimeter, were now confronted with the long trek to Dunkirk. For Private Edwin Newbould, the march was full of incident:

'We set off in good marching order but kept being held up by something at the front of the column. It was our elderly major who was meant to be in charge of us. He was apparently very drunk and kept falling down. There was little discipline anyway and the men showed scant regard for this regular officer. Insults were hurled at him. "You drunken old sod," "Stand up you old git," etc. Finally one of the NCOs said, "Let's leave the old bastard," and we did. His servant was one Charlie Flint and he stayed behind and brought him home safely. Flint stayed on with us but I never saw the Major again, although we were later told he had a nervous breakdown.'

Newbould remembers one scene on the march in particular:

'Halfway between La Panne and Dunkirk, I saw four soldiers, one to each corner of a blanket, carrying a lad who was wounded and appeared to be semi-conscious. They were continually trying to cheer him up. "Not far to go now," they'd say. I am sure they had carried him all the way from La Panne and it was still a considerable amount of miles before they would reach the jetty at Dunkirk, which was now becoming visible in the early morning light. It doesn't require much imagination to realize how cumbersome this burden must have been.'

Not all the wounded were so lucky. A number, along with the chronically fatigued, had little option but to stay where they were. However, by the end of the night the vast majority of troops had left the sands for the smoking town of Dunkirk, leaving the eastern beaches with an eerily quiet and deserted feel.

Further down the coast Walter Richardson, an NCO with the 21/Anti-Tank Regiment, prepared his men for the move to the pier. As they were about to set off his commanding officer assembled the soldiers and stated that a troop had to stay behind to cover the approaches to Bray Dunes, from the sea to the top of the cliff. It was a far from enviable task:

'I want a troop commander to stay behind with volunteers. "Well,

you're a single man, Mr Richardson. No doubt you will be volunteering." "It seems, sir, that I have no option," I replied, "so, thank you very much, I'll volunteer".'

It was not long before Richardson and his men were finding that the shelling was becoming more frequent and accurate. During a lull in the bombardment, they found a wireless set and heard Churchill's speech that 'the evacuation is now nearing completion. British troops have left the beaches'. 'It hardly instilled us with much confidence about our own plight,' he reflected later. Eventually Richardson and his unit did embark, but they were not the last of the BEF troops to leave the beaches. Captain Stephen Holloway woke up at dawn on 3 June on a beach littered with only discarded equipment and dead bodies. There was no sign of life anywhere:

'I must have been knocked out by a blast or just collapsed from sheer exhaustion. Anyway it soon became evident that I had been left for dead. After walking a considerable distance along the deserted beach, I eventually came across a Signals officer who had just destroyed the last telephone link with England. He informed me that there was nothing between ourselves and the German positions. This gave us a tremendous feeling of insecurity. We walked on and by luck came across what must have been the last Royal Navy party. They had no room on the boat, but towed us to a larger craft.'

It is reassuring to know that very few wounded British soldiers were left on the beaches. The Naval boat crews spent many hours 'sweeping' the coast before it fell to the Germans and any men still alive were rescued. Corporal Harry Dennis, East Surrey Regiment, was particularly grateful for the work of these sailors. Indeed, he could hardly believe his luck when he woke up to find himself in the relative comfort of a ship's cabin:

'"Where am I?", I asked, totally bewildered. "You're on the Albany and you're going back to Blighty," came the reply. I had no recollections from the time that I arrived on the beach but I must have gone unconscious as a result of a blast. Later, I was informed of what the sailors used to do. The ship would hove to off the coast and a few men would row ashore where they'd look at the bodies on the beach. If anybody was alive, they'd pick them up and take them back.'

Sadly, many thousands did die on the beaches. That the number was not higher was testament to the skill and determination of the Navy and civilian volunteers. They now had to turn their attention to the Dunkirk Mole, which was the only official means of embarkation from 1 June onward, although some still managed to evacuate troops from the shore nearby.

The evacuation from the beaches had been more successful than anyone had dared envisage, but the price in vessels and lives was high. For many of the weary troops returning to England there was little to celebrate. All had lost colleagues and a number suffered horrible guilt on account of their behaviour. This point was reinforced by one veteran I spoke to who told me about a good friend of his who committed suicide soon after as a result of what he had deemed to be his cowardly behaviour in rushing a boat.

There is little on and around the beaches now to remind us of the terror these soldiers were put through, and even if there was it is unlikely that we could ever fully empathize. As Gunner Albert 'Bunny' Burrow states:

'It must be realized that what happened on the beaches can never be shown, because if it was and people saw what really happened they would

German medical teams collected wounded from among the sand dunes.
TAYLOR LIBRARY

The Union Jack still flutters over this makeshift tent on the beach, despite the presence of victorious German troops. TAYLOR LIBRARY

be too shocked and upset. I know that many people who were on the beaches still have bad dreams about it all.'

Table of Troops Evacuated from the Beaches

Month	Amount of troops evacuated	Month	Amount of troops evacuated
May		June	
27	2,500	1	7,348
28	5,930	2	6,695
29	13,752	3	1,870
30	29,512	4	622
31	22,942		

What to see

La Panne Town Hall, a large modern building with flags outside it, stands back from Zeelaan Street. It houses the Tourist Information Centre which will provide detailed maps of the town. The staff are English-speaking and very helpful. There is also a plaque in the building which commemorates the evacuation. Opposite the Town Hall is the building, No. 16-18 Zeelaan, which was General Gort's last headquarters before he was evacuated back to England. The General stayed in the room behind the first floor bay window during a critical period of the operation. It proved an ideal location as there was a telephone cable running from the corner building direct to England.

One mile to the west is a sculpture commemorating the evacuation on Leopold I Esplanade. It is here that the Dunkirk veterans line up for a parade to remember the fallen during their annual pilgrimage. In front of this memorial is the large, imposing arch where the King's Summer Palace used to stand. Beneath it stands the statue of Leopold I, the first King of the Belgians, looking disdainfully towards the developments that increasingly encroach upon his space.

The beach itself is vast and one is instantly struck by its shallow gradient. It certainly illustrates the difficulty that boats must have encountered getting to the waiting troops. Deck chairs and sunbathing holidaymakers have replaced the weary, decimated troops who, in late May and early June 1940, so desperately prayed for salvation from the intense shelling and Stuka raids.

ıeral Gort's last HQ.

The La Panne communal Cemetery contains a number of Allied graves. Driving out along the Kerkstraat, watch for a sign. If you reach the roundabout you have gone too far. There is a car park just outside the cemetery. The CWGC cemetery is on the far left end as you enter. 281 men were buried here - including 4 Navy, 267 Army, 6 Airforce and 4 Merchant Navy. Of these 257 are British, 14 French, two Canadian and eight other Allied soldiers. Almost all died during the retreat to Dunkirk, but amongst the exceptions are two British servicemen from the First World War. Like all the Allied cemeteries in France/Belgium, it is well kept.

The Adinkerke Military Cemetery is harder to find with no clear sign to direct you. To locate it, head out of town along the Kerkstraat, which becomes La Pannelaan and then Stationstraat. On crossing over the canal, turn right at the roundabout along Dijk and then take the next left turning down Kromfortstraat. The cemetery is on your left very close to the motorway. Of the 365 men buried here, 142 are non-Commonwealth nationals. Most died in the First World War. Interestingly one grave, that of a certain Sabit Harun Mohammed – a member of the Egyptian Labour Corps – who was killed on 6 September, is separated from the rest. As at Furnes and many other cemeteries, there are a considerable number of Czech graves. With rows of German graves facing their side, it is a powerful reminder of the futility of war. Once foes, now resting in peace together.

Bray Dunes is considerably less commercial and sophisticated than La Panne, with none of the high-rise apartments that run along the latter's beachfront. There is not a lot to see but it is worth a wander along the vast, flat beach to understand how difficult the naval operation really was. Little remains to recall the incredible scenes that occurred in late May and early June 1940. On the beachfront, there is a large French memorial for the men of La 12ème Division D'Infanterie Motorisée, many of whom 'sacrificed their lives covering the embarkation of Allied troops'. To the left of it is a

The modest memorial on Leopold I Esplanade commemorating the extra-ordinary evacuation of Allied troops from France and Belgium in 1940.

small plaque for those who perished on the French destroyer Bourrasque, which was torpedoed on 30 May 1940.

'Where are the RAF?'

Al Deere's spitfire was shot down on beaches some fifteen miles from Dunkirk. After making his way to the port by foot and stolen bike, he attempted to board a destroyer but was prevented from doing so by a BEF major. Deere protested stating that he was an RAF pilot trying to get back to his squadron. The officer replied,

> *'I don't give a damn who you are. For all the good you chaps seem to be doing you might as well stay on the ground.'*

Deere embarked anyway and, on entering the ship's wardroom faced another cold reception from some more army officers. On enquiring as to what the RAF had done which was so wrong, one of the men replied, *'That's just it. What have you done?'*

The reaction of the major and the officers on the ship was mirrored by the BEF as a whole. Many soldiers believed that the 'Brylcreem boys' of the RAF had let them down by failing to provide adequate air support. From the beginning of the withdrawal to the evacuation itself, the men on the ground justifiably questioned the number of Allied planes employed in France. The French themselves were upset by the RAF's apparent lack of involvement. Following the fall of Sedan on 15 May, their Prime Minister Paul Reynaud had urged Churchill to send as many aircraft as possible. Churchill would have done so but was outvoted by the War Cabinet which had been lobbied by Air Chief Marshal Sir Hugh Dowding. Dowding argued that Britain could not afford to send any more fighter aircraft, as they had already lost too many and the remainder were needed for the coming defence of the island. The government, which had shown itself utterly complacent in speeding up aircraft production during the phoney war, now paid the price for ineptitude and agreed.

Sir Hugh Dowding

Even when 'Operation Dynamo' started, Dowding continued to argue that the bulk of the RAF should not be risked. His refusal to allow Fighter Command's defensive strength to fall below the 'indispensable minimum' of twenty-five squadrons left Air Vice Marshal Keith Park, who was responsible for providing air cover over Dunkirk and the channel, with just sixteen squadrons (200 planes) to work with. It was an impossible task, not least

A group of German NCOs pose on the nose of a downed Hurricane. The RAF were unable to prevent the Luftwaffe from getting through to the crowded beaches.

because in the early days of evacuation his fighter planes were also required to protect the British aircraft dropping supplies over Calais. News of the garrison's surrender on 26 May did not reach Park for a day and a number of his planes were used on futile missions on the 27th, unaware that the packages of food and ammunition were dropping straight into enemy hands.

Park's initial strategy was to try and provide almost continuous cover over Dunkirk and the surrounding area. This was no easy task as the Hurricanes and Spitfires, flying from bases some eighty kilometres away in Kent, had fuel tanks which restricted them to less than half an hour's patrol over the beaches. This meant that Park had to spread his planes lightly, and rarely in the early days of rescue would more than a squadron (twelve planes) be in the air at the same time. The drawbacks of this strategy soon became all too apparent whenever these small teams met the enemy, who flew in much greater numbers (one German raid on 28 May consisted of 140 Stukas and 200 other aircraft). The dogfights that ensued in the early days of the evacuation were hardly fair contests and the RAF suffered considerable losses. On 27 May, for example, the eleven Spitfires of No. 754 Squadron faced thirty Dornier 17s and Messerschmitt 109s, and later that day twenty Hurricanes were forced to do battle with approximately forty Messerschmitt 119s. Unsurprisingly, little was effectively done to halt these great waves of enemy aircraft, which were causing such havoc to the men on the beaches and port.

On 29 May tactics were changed. It was decided that fewer, but stronger, patrols would have greater success in deterring enemy air activity. Instead of flying twenty-three numerically weak sorties, Park ordered just nine, but with two or three squadrons in each. The obvious disadvantage was that the Luftwaffe faced little opposition for extended periods during the day and had an uncanny knowledge of those moments when the beaches were without fighter protection.

One piece of encouragement for the men at Fighter Command Headquarters was that their new fighter, the Spitfire, stood up extremely well against the Messerschmitt 109s and 110s. They soon proved more versatile than their counterparts, making sharper turns and holding a dive for longer. The RAF's other modern fighter, the Hurricane, also proved more than equal to the best the Luftwaffe offered. Many German airmen found their first experience of meeting the new aircraft a terrifying one. A Stuka pilot, Rudolf Braun recalled, *'From the British fighters we met heavy resistance'*, whilst Major Werner Kneipe reported back, having lost six of the Dorniers in his squadron, that 'The enemy pounced on our tightly knit formation with maniacal fury'.

Such comments suggest that the RAF put up much more of a fight than the soldiers gave it credit for. Yet, whilst it seems that the British squadrons did cause the enemy anxieties, the problem was that their limited numbers ensured that such occurrences were all too rare. Nonetheless, it was at Dunkirk that the Luftwaffe pilots first realized that air superiority was not solely a German preserve.

Throughout this time the RAF attempted to further this point by wildly exaggerating their success rate. On 27 May they lost fourteen fighters but claimed that thirty-eight enemy planes were shot down. An examination of Luftwaffe records reveals that they only lost ten. On 1 June the RAF initially claimed seventy-eight, a number they later reduced to forty-three as a result of double counting. In fact the Germans lost just twenty-nine, of which a number were brought down by anti-aircraft fire. That same day the RAF lost thirty-one. Churchill attempted to make the most of the British successes and at one point during the evacuation he even claimed that six German machines were being brought down for every British one. Not only was such a statement deliberately misleading, it was also blatantly untrue, as the RAF were suffering more losses than anyone dared admit.

This was hardly surprising, as the Luftwaffe had already seen action in the Spanish Civil War (1936-39) and the Polish invasion. The experience the

German airmen had gained in these conflicts contrasted sharply with their British counterparts. Indeed a number of Spitfire pilots at Dunkirk had rarely ever flown one before and, understandably, took some time to adjust to the sophisticated controls and equipment of these new machines. Squadron Leader James 'The Prof' Leathart was all too aware of this dearth of skilled pilots.

> *'They were often very inexperienced. Most had done no more than five hours in Spits and had never even fired their guns. I knew it was murder to send them off with no training.'*

Leathart's instincts proved correct and many never returned. Most were, of course, shot down by German planes, but some were victims of 'friendly' fire. Indeed, a number of incidents were cited of Spitfires mistaking Hurricanes for enemy aircraft. Nevertheless, the fighting provided pilots with some much-needed experience which was to hold them in good stead when they faced the enemy again during the Battle of Britain. Indeed, it was above the beaches that future flying aces like Douglas Bader were first blooded.

Douglas Bader CBE, DSO, DFC.

An extract from his biography *Reach for the Sky* describes his first kill, whilst also capturing the intensity of the dogfights that occurred over Dunkirk;

> *'The 110s wheeled inland without dropping their bombs, but the sky was empty of cloud and the Spitfires leapt after them, blaring on full throttle. No time for thinking, but as he turned his reflector sight on the gun button to 'fire', he knew he was going to shoot. A glance back through the Perspex, the straining Spitfires were stringing out in a ragged line and up to the left four grey shapes were diving at them – Messerschmitt 109s, the first he had seen. From the beam they flicked across in front like darting sharks, winking orange flashes in the noses as they fired.*
>
> *He rammed stick and rudder over and the Spitfire wheeled after them. A 109 shot up in front; his thumb jabbed the firing button and the guns in the wings squirted with a shocking noise. The 109 seemed to be filling his windscreen. A puff of white spurted just behind its cockpit as though someone had used a giant Flit-gun. The puff was chopped off... for a moment nothing... then a spurt of orange flame mushroomed round the cockpit and flared back like a blow-torch. The 109 rolled drunkenly showing her belly, and in the same moment he saw the black cross on its side. It was true. They did have black crosses.*

Suddenly it was real and the 109 was falling away and behind flaming.'

These dogfights were certainly not for the fainthearted and the bravery of the pilots, who flew as many as four of these hazardous sorties a day, is undeniable. A letter written by Flight Lieutenant R.D.G. Wright of 213 Squadron on 31 May epitomizes their spirit and commitment.

'Well another day is gone, and with it a lot of grand blokes. Got another brace of 109s today, but the whole Luftwaffe seemed to leap on us – we were hopelessly outnumbered. I was caught napping by a 109 in the middle of a dog-fight, and got a couple of holes in the aircraft, one of them filled the office with smoke, but the Jerry overshot and he's dead. If anyone says anything to you in the future about the inefficiency of the RAF – I believe the BEF troops were booing the RAF in Dover the other day – tell them from me we only wish we could do more. But without aircraft we can do no more than we have done – that is, our best, and it's fifty times better than the Germans' best, though they are fighting under the most advantageous conditions. So don't worry, we are going to win this war even if we have only one aeroplane and one pilot left – the Boche could produce the whole Luftwaffe and you would see the one pilot and the one aeroplane go into combat.'

Stories of heroism abound. James Leathart was leading No 54 Squadron when he saw a Spitfire going down at March airfield, on the edge of Calais. On returning to base he learned that Squadron Leader Drogo White, the Commander of the No 74 Squadron was missing. Leathart at once set off back to Calais in search of him, flying an unarmed Miles Master two-seater trainer, and escorted by his flight commanders, the New Zealander Al Deere and Johnny Allen. After landing, Leathart could see no sign of White, and so took off to rejoin his escort. He had reached 1,000 feet when Deere yelled *'Messerschmitts!'* Leathart headed for the safety of the ground

An RAF Hudson bomber provides some protection close to the English coastline.

and, as soon as he had landed, jumped into a ditch. To his astonishment he almost fell on top of the missing White, who was hiding from some German tanks. The Luftwaffe somehow failed to spot the bright orange Master trainer and, after cranking the engine manually, the pair headed home. Shortly afterwards, King George VI visited the Spitfire wing at Hornchurch to present Leathart with his DSO.

Despite such examples of individual and collective heroism, the RAF undoubtedly struggled at Dunkirk. With the benefit of hindsight, Dowding's decision to preserve the bulk of his force for the coming defence of Britain was probably the right one. It was, however, a massive gamble, not least because it seems highly unlikely that the war could have continued without the BEF. Furthermore, the decision caused widespread resentment among soldiers who understandably felt that they deserved greater protection from the murderous Luftwaffe raids. The RAF was however, more active than some troops perceived and much of the fighting would have occurred out of sight. For example, whilst some on the beaches may have observed sporadic bombing of German position, few would have known that every day fifty Blenheims attacked enemy formations and hindered their advance by bombing the roads, railways and bridges leading up to the port. Nevertheless, the RAF could have been much more active and no amount of oratorical bluster from Churchill could conceal this fact. Many soldiers actually recall finding it difficult hearing their Prime Minister telling the nation that *'Hour after hour the RAF bit into the German fighters and bombers'* when they had witnessed little or no activity themselves. The RAF clearly did not achieve a victory at that time. Their finest hour was yet to come.

CHAPTER SIX

DUNKIRK and THE MOLE

From Bray Dunes, Dunkirk is a short drive along the N1/D940. The city centre is well signposted and provides a good starting point. Like all ports, the docks and harbour areas are heavily industrialized and not attractive. However, the town centre itself is surprisingly pleasant with restaurants and hotels near, or overlooking, the Place de Jean Bart.

A burnt-out British truck in Place Jean Bart facing the tower of Saint Eloi Church. TAYLOR LIBRARY

'Bloody Monday'

It is hardly surprising that Dunkirk has changed so much since 1940 given the massive amount of raids it endured during the evacuation of the BEF that year. On 27 May, a day that came to be known as 'Bloody Monday', Göring's 2nd and 3rd Air Fleets dropped more than 2,000 tons of high explosive bombs on the town, reducing much of it to rubble. 30,000 incendiaries added to the devastation a little later in the afternoon. As the water mains had burst the day before, the fire brigade was forced to use sea water which they pumped from the harbour as a last-ditch attempt to impede the rampant flames from inflicting further damage. Some areas, like Place de Jean Bart, were partially saved but much of Dunkirk, including the famous 15th century Church of St. Eloi, was left a smouldering ruin. Civilian casualties were high, with over one thousand dead on this day alone.

For the majority of troops in the town, it was a matter of trying to find any safe refuge from this terrible bombing. Second Lieutenant Anthony Rhodes of the Royal Horse Artillery arrived in Dunkirk as the Luftwaffe raid began and soon found himself sheltering in a cellar:

> *'By midday the cellar was becoming rather smelly, it held sixty men only with difficulty. Many of them did not bother to come up for air during the intervals (between air raids), and it soon took on that musty, military smell, so much part of an army. It was not improved by a well-intentioned soldier who had given some foie-gras to one of the stray dogs which had taken refuge with us; it promptly vomited in the corner on somebody's gas mask. By four in the afternoon our nerves were becoming a little frayed. One of the NCOs (wearing last-war ribbons) was crying quietly in the corner and several men began to make queer little animal noises – rather like homesick dogs. This was understandable because, as the raids repeated, they seemed to have a sort of cumulative effect on one's system; after a while the mere thought of a raid was worse than its reality.'*

When Rhodes, and other soldiers, emerged from their shelter, the town was unrecognizable from the one he had arrived in only hours before. Major Adair of the Grenadier Guards recalls:

> *'The destruction was ghastly. Scarcely a building remained untouched and the debris and litter made progress difficult. There was no opportunity to clear up the streets or bury the dead.'*

Later Civil Defence workers did begin the unpleasant task of collecting the dead and wounded from the debris-strewn streets. Their findings made sorry reading:

> *'Unknown infant, sex male, age about two years, dressed in white shawl, a blue and white vest, two white woollen vests, a red sweater, and wrapped in a black woollen shawl.'*
>
> *'Unknown infant, undetermined sex, about ten years of age, dressed in*

German reconnaissance troops amongst the smoking ruins of Dunkirk.

a blue jacket belonging to a sailor costume with white buttons.'

'Unknown man, one metre 75 centimetres tall, strongly built, bandage on left foot and thigh, wrapped in sheet.'

'Unknown woman, in state of pregnancy (five to six months).'

'Unknown, undetermined sex, aged between sixteen and eighteen years...'

Vitally for the evacuation, which had only properly begun that day, the port was terribly damaged. Captain William Tennant, the Senior Naval Officer at Dunkirk, who had been sent over by Admiral Ramsay, concluded that the harbour area could no longer be used, 'Port continuously bombed all day and on fire. Embarkation possible only from beaches east of the harbour. Send all ships there.'

This was a major setback. Troops were already being lifted far too slowly from the beaches. There were few small boats, and these were already struggling with the long distances they had to be rowed to and from their parent ships. It was taking many hours to fill these waiting ships which were, to all intents and purposes, 'sitting ducks' for the rampant Luftwaffe. Tennant knew that, if the docks were operational, embarkations would be around ten times faster. They were not, though, and ideas were fast running out.

The Mole

At around midnight Tennant and two of his officers decided to survey the two Moles that formed the entrance to the harbour. To his amazement, whilst Dunkirk's quays were ablaze, these breakwaters remained untouched by the Luftwaffe bombs.

'Here's something quicker – if only we could get a ship alongside,' he said,

'Well, we'll try it – tell that nearest one to come alongside.'

Tennant knew that attempting to use the East Mole was a wild stab in the dark. It seemed highly unlikely that this concrete-piled structure with a flimsy wooden walkway could withstand the buffeting it would receive from a ship sliding up against it. One thing was certain – superb seamanship would be required. The Moles had never been intended as loading bays. They were open at the sides to allow the sea to pass through and at high tide with strong winds it would surge through and over the wooden staging. A further hindrance to embarkation was that, while this eastern jetty ran some 1,600 yards out to sea, it was far from wide. A maximum of three men abreast could walk along it at one time and this seemed destined to cause congestion. The Mole did, however, provide Tennant with a glimmer of hope and, as the deliverance of the BEF was in his hands, he had little choice but to gamble on it.

The passenger steamer, *Queen of the Channel* was the first to attempt the desperately risky operation. Tension ran high as First Captain W.J. Odell eased her bow in at a gingerly six knots. A head rope was made just as the ship's stern eased gently in to nudge against the mole. Within minutes the *Queen of the Channel* was secured. Tennant was able to breath a sigh of relief as the heavy clump of army boots made its way towards him. The first contingents were under way and less than an hour later the passenger ship departed with 950 men aboard.

Spirits were now lifted as increasing numbers of ships began lining up along the breakwater. There was further good news as dawn broke the next day. Misty conditions and thick smoke obscured the Luftwaffe's view of the Mole. Major Allan Younger explains:

> *'To the west end of Dunkirk some oil storage drums and tanks had been set on fire. A vast plume of black smoke was being blown exactly along the harbour. German aircraft had little option but to just toss bombs through the smoke, without knowing what they were aiming for.'*

On 28 May some 11,874 soldiers were lifted off the Mole. It was still far too few but as organization was stepped up so the rates of embarkation began to rise. Soon, long lines of troops, three abreast were being efficiently lifted off. Chief Petty Officer Oliver Anderson, serving aboard HMS *Sutton*, was impressed with the order of the men as his ship first sidled up to the Mole:

> *'The Navy party ashore were really organized. As soon as we got alongside, troops formed up and made their way along the jetty. This was just as well because the air raids were getting really worrisome and we didn't want to hang around. It only took us half an hour before we were loaded!'*

The fact that it became possible to pack up to 600 men on to the crammed decks of an armed ship in less than twenty minutes was, to a large extent,

An armed trawler lies on the bottom next to the Mole. Behind is the Destroyer HMS *Vivacious* loading up with troops.

Oil storage tanks ablaze to the west of the town of Dunkirk. The palls of smoke did much to shield Allied troops and ships from the rampant Luftwaffe.

down to the work of one man. Commander Jack Clouston was a tough Canadian who had been sent over by Admiral Ramsay to act as piermaster. His job entailed efficiently embarking the crowds of chaotic bodies that had amassed around the harbour. As these crowds grew, so the task became more difficult. It could have been likened to getting an entire football crowd through one turnstile. He managed it by putting army officers under his control, who were then ordered to prepare groups of men, by fifties, to dash at the word of command along the Mole, where a party of naval officers would direct the troops to their allocated ships.

Some soldiers were overeager to get to the ships that promised their salvation. A number broke ranks and rushed on to any vessel they could. Such lapses of discipline were not tolerated and, in this pressured environment, naval officers took firm action to prevent chaos breaking out. Peter Wells was an eyewitness to an incident involving a French Officer;

> *'A Royal Naval destroyer, the Caprice, was taking some French troops. All of a sudden a French officer started to rush up the gangway. A naval Lieutenant ordered him to stop and join his troops in single file. Such was the panic of the officer that he continued to run. The Lieutenant promptly drew his pistol and shot him dead as he was half-way up the bow.'*

On the whole the discipline was first rate. Lieutenant Colonel P B Longdon, a surgeon on HMS *Anthony,* recalls watching some guardsmen embark:

> *'We went straight into the Mole at Dunkirk, which was under fire from*

the Germans, and took off what was left of the Guards. They marched down the pier in threes and in perfect step. The NCO said, "Guards, 'alt, Guards left turn, Guards will embark", I think there were about 1,000 of them and they embarked in about 20 minutes.'

On arrival at Dover the next day, after a series of near-misses, he remembers that they then:

'Paraded on the quay side and marched off to the trains. Unshaven, tired out, very strained, indeed with rifles spotless. In my opinion, the finest soldiers in the world.'

Few vessels could gauge their own capacity and it was up to the embarkation teams to make the utmost use of them. When Lieutenant R.C. Watkin on the destroyer *Winchelsea* jumped ashore and told Clouston the ship could take four hundred, the piermaster was scathing:

'Come back and tell me when you've got a thousand.'

To Watkin's astonishment the Tommies did squeeze in somehow, but in doing so were forced to part with their equipment, including their rifles, which were all thrown into the sea in order to maximize the spaces on the ships.

Attacks on the Mole were becoming more and more frequent. Sailors disliked using it as their ships were extremely vulnerable targets while tied up. Even though it took longer, many preferred embarking troops from the beaches. Mr S Payne, once a young signalman on HMS *Vega*, explains why:

'Lifting troops off the mole entailed ships going alongside, securing bow and stern and, when fully loaded, coming out astern, turning and making for home. A lengthy manoeuvre, plus the fact that the Mole made an ideal aiming point for the droves of JU 87s which came over from dawn to dusk. There were many soldiers who with rescue at their fingertips bought it on that Mole; sailors too of course. HMS Imogen received a bomb which went straight down her funnel as she was leaving the Mole loaded with troops. She literally disintegrated... We hated the Mole. To us it was just a question of time before a bomb with our number on it was dropped.'

Up until now, the main threat to the Mole came from shells fired from just beyond the French-held Mardyck fort, some seven miles away. The weather had been kind to the evacuees, with poor visibility from the smoke and steady drizzle threatening to make Göring's promise that the Luftwaffe would finish off the BEF an empty one.

However, on the afternoon of 29 May, a fresh northern wind blew the smoke clear of the port. Suddenly the Mole looked more vulnerable than ever. It did not take long for the Germans to take full advantage of this change of fortune. A massive air raid involving 400 aircraft and led by 180 Stukas was launched.

The attack began at the worst possible moment with eight destroyers, one passenger ship, two minesweepers and six trawlers lying alongside the

Mole. The destroyer HMS *Grenade* received two direct hits and, within minutes, *Fenella*, a wooden steamer, became the next victim, followed soon after by the minesweeper *Calvi* and two trawlers. Amidst the terrible noise and sights around them, Commander Clouston's men loosed the ships' lines so that they would not go down at their berth. The remaining trawlers towed *Grenade* away but were unable to save *Fenella* and *Calvi*. Bombs were raining down as they frantically worked to clear the harbour of wreckage. Stanley Allen found himself full of admiration for these trawler men:

> *'It really was incredible how they managed to clear the damaged ships and debris from their berths. This was fantastically brave work as they were sitting ducks to the aircraft. For the Luftwaffe pilots, it must have been plain target practice because of the terrific sighting the line to the East Mole gave them.'*

During the raid some of the soldiers on the seaward end of the Mole began to panic. So intense was the bombing on the pier that a number simply jumped into the sea. Others tried to move back down towards land. They were met by Commander Clouston with his revolver drawn. Quietly but firmly, he spoke to them,

> *'We have come to take you back to the UK. I have six bullets and I am not a bad shot. The Lieutenant behind me is an even better one. So that makes twelve of you.'*

He paused and then bellowed, *'Now get into those bloody ships!'* They obliged.

When calm returned, it became clear that the air attack had been a truly devastating one, not just around the harbour but also elsewhere. In all, four destroyers were sunk, as were a number of other vessels including the *Clan MacAllister*, a 6,000 ton cargo liner loaded with eight assault landing craft. The Mole itself, which had led a charmed life until now, received a number of hits. Though damaged, miraculously it was still usable and Clouston's men did as much as they could to fill in the craters.

Unfortunately, at this point embarkation from the still operational Mole ceased. This was due to a message received by Admiral Ramsay at the Dynamo Room at Dover in which a Naval Commander on shore patrol duties at La Panne had claimed, without authority, that the harbour was completely blocked as a result of the raid. Evacuation, the Commander stated, must now become a purely beach affair. Ramsay accepted this message with anguish and signalled:

> *'All ships approaching Dunkirk will not, repeat not, approach the harbour. Remain instead off the eastern beach to collect troops from the shore.'*

Inexplicably neither Tennant nor Ramsay ever received each other's signals and during the night of 29 May virtually no troops were lifted off the Mole, when an estimated 15,000 could have been embarked. Admiral

Groups of men were organized and then, between raids, dashed along the Mole where they crossed over on make-shift gang planks to the waiting ships. Embarkation, as the photograph shows, was a hazardous business for the exhausted soldiers.

Wake-Walker, sent the next day to speed up the evacuation, later reflected on the effects of the Commander's mistake:

'It took two days to overcome the result of this indiscretion which had considerable temporary effect on the plans.'

Admiral Ramsay had further problems to deal with. The First Sea Lord, Admiral Sir Dudley Pound, argued that the Naval losses were getting too high and recalled the eight most modern destroyers in the evacuation fleet, believing that the destroyers' first duty was to protect Britain's sea lifeline. It was a decision that Ramsay was vehemently opposed to as the fifteen old destroyers left to him could lift only 17,000 in the next twenty-four hours.

By noon of 30 May the Mole was at least being utilized, but still too few ships approached it and the numbers embarking were disappointingly low. Ironically, the Luftwaffe, believing the port to be fully closed, barely attacked it that day and the thick mist ensured they never knew otherwise. Ernest Long arrived soon after the bombing raid and describes the scene around the harbour at this time:

'I could see the masts of sunken ships all over the harbour. Some had

been blasted onto the beach, and there was evidence of aircraft dogfights with parts of shot-down planes of both sides littering the sands. There were hastily prepared slit trenches dug by those who had preceded us and in quite a lot of these trenches were dead bodies of those who had been killed by enemy action. It was a terrible gruesome sight. The harbour master and his assistants were trying desperately hard to organize the embarking troops into any boat or ship that had managed to reach the side of the Mole. When my turn came I remember having to balance across a gangplank that had been put across a part of the Mole that had received a direct hit. That hit had left a wide gap between the two sections. I remember seeing the bodies of several Guardsmen who had been caught in the bombing and they were lying along the edge of the Mole. Whether they were ever shipped back for burial I'll never know. In the dock area of the town black smoke was pouring from the fuel tanks that had been set on fire, adding to the devastation around us.'

Embarkation following the air attack was now more hazardous for all concerned. Not only did troops have to walk perilously along hastily improvised wooden planks at various points down the Mole, but the forest of sunken masts and superstructures in the harbour made the ships' approach a navigator's nightmare. Even when alongside the Mole it was by no means easy to embark due to a fifteen-foot rise and fall of tide. Ladders were used where possible but some men found themselves having to shimmy down telegraph posts, whilst the troops lifted off by the destroyer HMS *Icarus* used water-polo goalposts

Despite such hindrances, numbers of troops lifted off somehow increased dramatically. On 31 May records show 45,072 soldiers embarked from the pier and its importance was heightened with the news that the perimeter was fast shrinking. Time was running out and a number of Generals received individual orders from London to return immediately.

All quiet along the Mole.

The Generals Depart - Reputations Lost and Made

General Alan Brooke

Throughout the week of 28 May to 2 June the Generals themselves began to evacuate. The massive amount of responsibility and organization heaped on their shoulders since the German invasion had begun, rendered most of them utterly exhausted. The first to depart was General Pownall on the evening of 29 May. Lieutenant General Brooke, ordered by the War Office to leave the next day, clearly felt in a dilemma:

> *'After having struggled with the Corps through all its vicissitudes, and having guided it to the sea, I felt a deserter not remaining with it until the last.'*

His emotions ran high as he prepared to embark. Whether it was the tragedy of the BEF or just sheer tension after such a test of his distinguished leadership, Brooke gave way to tears in front of Monty, the man taking over his Corps. Montgomery, who had the utmost respect for this normally reserved and austere commander, recalled,

> *'I saw that he was struggling to hold himself in check so I took him a little way into the sand dunes and then he broke down and wept.'*

Lord Gort VC

Lord Gort, in keeping with his character, was absolutely determined not to leave until the entire BEF had been evacuated. Major Stanley Hill was serving as a Staff Officer at the General's Headquarters in La Panne when he stated his intention to stay:

> *'He said, "I've been the Commander of this army and it's going back. I'm certainly not going back with it. I'm going to end my days with the last of the troops".'*

Lord Munster, returning from the beaches, informed Churchill, who was in the bath at the time, of Gort's decision. Churchill was appalled. Gort must return, he insisted, as it was unfeasible to hand the Germans a propaganda coup, which the capture of the British Commander-in-Chief would undoubtedly have been. After a brief meeting with Eden, Churchill scribbled on his hand an order that left Gort with no option but to comply:

> *'If we can still communicate we shall send you an order to return to England with such officers as you may choose at the moment when we deem your command so reduced that it can be handed over to a Corps Commander. You should now nominate this Commander. If communications are broken, you are to hand over and return as specified when your effective fighting force does not exceed the equivalent of three*

divisions. This is in accordance with correct military procedure, and no personal discretion is left you in the matter.'

The most obvious choice of successor was General Michael Barker commanding I Corps, as his men would be the last to embark. Montgomery clearly believed Barker was not the man for the job, describing him as 'an utterly useless commander who had lost his nerve by 30 May.' His assessment was almost certainly based on Barker's conduct at a GHQ conference when, as expected, he was nominated by Gort to take his job. No sooner was the meeting over than Barker, storming out of the room, cried, 'Why has this responsibility been thrust upon me?' Montgomery lingered for a chat with Gort and soon expressed his opinion that Barker was no longer fit to command. Whilst Gort is unlikely to have been persuaded by the views of a junior officer, he had doubts himself and decided to appoint Major General Harold Alexander. 'Alex', an Irish Guards Officer, had displayed a toughness and coolness under pressure that made him an ideal candidate for the job.

ajor General Harold Alexander

ajor General Bernard Montgomery

On the afternoon of 31 May Lord Gort, having carefully cut the medal ribbons from his spare uniforms, was ferried out to the destroyer HMS *Hebe*. It was a far from distinguished departure for the man who, by this stage, had already saved half the BEF through his decision to evacuate.

Dunkirk was the making of a number of generals' careers, most notably Brooke's, Alexander's and Montgomery's. Monty, who left Dunkirk a day after Gort, had excelled throughout the campaign. Abrasive and conceited, he had few friends but many admirers. By the time he stepped off the Mole, he had proved beyond doubt his ability as a military commander. During the withdrawal he had directed a particularly difficult manoeuvre, moving 3 Division, comprising 13,000 men, some 25 miles before slipping them into the large gap on the northern side of the Allied pocket. Due to this massive sidestep, the eastern wall of the escape corridor was covered. The move, done at night along back lanes and unfamiliar roads with the enemy often within two miles of his troops, had only been possible as a result of the training and drilling he had insisted on during the Phoney War.

Alexander's appointment by Gort to be his successor highlights the impression he too had made over the proceeding days and months in France. Monty and Alex had very different qualities, but General Brooke, their Corps Commander, spoke of them in equally glowing terms and realized their importance in Britain's future war efforts:

'In taking over the 1st Division I was for the first time having the experience of having Alexander working under me. It was a great opportunity... to see what he was made of, and what an admirable commander he was when in a tight place. It was intensely interesting watching him and Monty during those trying days, both of them completely imperturbable and efficiency itself, and yet two totally different characters. Monty with his quick brain for appreciating military situations was well aware of the very critical situation that he was in, and the very dangers and difficulties that faced us acted as a stimulus on him; they thrilled him and put the sharpest of edges on his military ability. Alex, on the other hand, gave me the impression of never fully realizing all the very unpleasant potentialities of our predicament. He remained entirely unaffected by it, completely composed and appeared never to have the slightest doubt that all would come right in the end. It was in those critical days that the appreciation I made of those two commanders remained rooted in my mind and resulted in the future selection of these two men to work together in the triumphal advance from Alamein to Tunis.'

Brooke himself impressed his troops and fellow generals with his utter professionalism. Lieutenant Colonel Brian Horrocks, (later Lieutenant General) reflected later about the qualities of his Corps Commander at Dunkirk:

'The more I have studied this campaign the clearer it becomes that the man who really saved the BEF was Lieutenant General A F Brooke (later Viscount Alanbrooke). I felt vaguely at the time that this alert, seemingly iron man without a nerve in his body, whom I met from time to time at 3rd Division Headquarters and who gave out his orders in short, clipped sentences, was a great soldier, but it is only now that I realize fully just how great he was. We regarded him as a highly efficient military machine. It is only since I have read his diaries that I appreciate what a consummate actor he must have been. Behind the confident mask was a sensitive nature of a man who hated war, the family man-cum-bird-watcher, in fact. Yet he never gave us the slightest indication of those moments of utter despair when it seemed to him almost impossible that any of us would ever escape.'

For some senior officers, such as Michael Barker, the events between 10 May and 4 June proved their undoing. He retired from the army after Dunkirk and died in obscurity in 1946. Lord Gort's reputation also seems to have suffered unjustly and the whole experience of organizing the withdrawal left him shattered. It was to be his last fighting command. His next post was as Governor General of Malta, and he ended his career as High Commissioner in Palestine, where he died soon after the war ended aged sixty.

The Mole Alone

Major General Alexander, Gort's successor, was instantly thrown into some tricky diplomatic talks with his French counterparts. It had become apparent to them that a massive discrepancy was developing over the nationality of the troops evacuating. Indeed by 31 May, of a total of 165,000 evacuated, only some 15,000 were French soldiers, none of whom had used the Mole. Churchill, recognizing the potential long-term harm to relations between the two countries that this grievance might cause, stepped in and promised the proportions would be equalized. At 8.15pm, Eden, the Secretary of State for War, wired Alexander an urgent message:

'You should withdraw your force as rapidly as possible on a 50-50 basis

Some French troops along with the Tommies arrive safely in England.

with the French Army, aiming at completion by night of 1-2 June. You should inform the French of this definite instruction.'

By 1 June the town heaved with civilians and Allied troops, many of whom had been forced to make the ten-mile march from La Panne. Seven times more men embarked from the Mole than the beaches that day.

Whilst the number of troops in Dunkirk was dwindling all the time, the same cannot be said of the canine population. Many servicemen befriended these frightened animals and thoroughly disliked the treatment they received at the hands of the military police. A spectator to these bizarre scenes was Ian Nethercroft aboard HMS *Keith.*

'A number of troops had dogs which they'd picked up. Indeed there were dogs everywhere. Military police were shooting them and throwing them into the harbour. Every time they did so, there was a big "boo" from all the sailors on the ships.'

If such incidents affected the troops' morale, so too did rumours that the perimeter was fast crumbling. News that a number of Germans had somehow managed to infiltrate into the centre of the town soon spread to the soldiers in the harbour and confirmed that the Allies' desperate defence of the bridgehead was coming to an end. Several hundred Guardsmen decided to take the matter in hand and launch a surprise bayonet attack on these unwanted arrivals. Edgar Rabbets, 5/Northants, volunteered to take part in this quarter- mile charge through the town, which finished up in the main square, Place de Jean Bart.

'I only used my bayonet on one man. My short legs found it hard to keep up with the Guardsmen and I just used the bayonet on the first German I came across. I got him right in the middle. There was no messing with those big bayonets. When you jab one of them in and twist it, they don't live. The charge was a complete success, as the Germans obviously hadn't expected anything of this sort to happen. We managed to clear the whole area which gave everybody in the docks a little bit of breathing space.'

Life in a Dunkirk Hospital

Other heroics were being performed by medical staff who attended to the mass of wounded in horrific conditions. One of these men was Lawrence Edwards, an NCO Nursing Orderly, who had spent the past week or ten days in an improvised hospital in a château on the eastern outskirts of Dunkirk. It was a far from ideal place to treat the hordes of wounded men who required urgent attention.

Lawrence Edwards

'Already when we moved in, it was little more than a shell. There were holes in the roof, no glass in the windows, no water in the taps and no power in the electric wires. In the lowest cellar of our mansion we found an ancient iron pump, which when

A French soldier awaits treatment.

energetically cranked would yield a thin stream of blackish, greenish water, and most of the time this was all we had for our medical and culinary use. The Colonel allocated one of the best downstairs rooms for the operating theatre. Since there was no glass in the windows the only way to keep out the dust of the outside world was to close the shutters, mercifully still intact. We drove one of our trucks up to the window, took off one headlamp and brought this into the theatre on the end of a long lead. All the nursing orderlies were fully employed elsewhere, so the driver was detailed to hold the lamps over the surgeon's busy fingers. Alas, he had never seen sights like this; in the middle of the first operation he fainted and the lamp clattered down on to the patient.'

Edwards and the rest of the nursing staff had to survive on virtually no sleep, as casualties from the battlefields, beaches and Mole flooded in. He had only eight months of medical experience. His orderlies, young ex-coalminers from Birmingham, had less than half that much. Yet no amount of training could have prepared them for the nightmarish conditions they were working under.

'I was busy in another part of the building supervising the intake of what seemed like an endless stream of wounded. Never had I seen such a concentration of bruised and broken bodies. Most had been lying in the field for many hours, some for days, without medical attention. Never did I see such obstinate determination to stay cheerful. Never did I hear a word of complaint or self-pity. I said to myself, "Whatever happens to me after this, I will never complain about my life again," a resolution which, alas, I have not kept during these fifty years as well as I ought!

I saw our officers (the doctors) worked up to, and sometimes almost beyond, the point of breakdown. I saw our orderlies trudging in and out, in and out, with the endless train of stretchers, while almost asleep on their feet. Soon every square foot of floor space was taken up by the rows of stretchers.'

Without adequate supplies of staff and equipment, standard medical practice had to be forfeited. The orderlies just had to do the best they could to ease the suffering of the crowds of wounded.

'I saw two young nursing orderlies, only lately from the mines. They had armed themselves with the largest syringes they could find and charged them with enough morphia to poison half a regiment. Nothing was under lock and key: we had no locks or keys! They were going up and down the serried ranks of stretchers giving a jab here and a jab there, wherever they thought they found human suffering coming to the point of culmination. Ought I to have reprimanded them and taken the syringes away? I found that I didn't have it in my heart to do so. I don't think they killed or seriously harmed anyone: and they certainly saved a lot of suffering. Sometimes it is better to look the other way.'

By 2 June everyone in the hospital knew that the evacuation of troops was coming to a close. With the enemy guns becoming louder as the perimeter shrunk, it was clear that a decision as to whether they should leave or stay would have to be addressed.

'We were all summoned to the basement of our château. The Sergeant Major was there, with his tin hat under his arm. He looked grim. He explained that the last hospital ship had left for home. The evacuation was finishing that night. One more ship, with good fortune, was due to leave. Our unit had been promised places on it. But High Command had ordained that for every hundred wounded which we would leave behind, ten orderlies and one officer must stay and be taken prisoner with them. Out of a hundred of us, thirty must stay. "Now look 'ere: I've got a 'undred pieces of screwed up paper in my 'elmet 'ere: thirty of them has got crosses on them: you comes up 'ere, you takes your piece of paper: and if it's got a cross on it, then Gawd 'elp yer - ye're for it!" '

Loss of sleep undermines one's power of judgement. The rumour had spread that the Germans were taking so many prisoners that they were standing them against a wall and shooting them rather than having the burden of feeding them. In our rundown state perhaps we half believed it. It was a tense moment, fumbling in that tin hat for one's piece of paper. I was lucky.'

The Last Days

By 2 June the Navy was paying a terrible price for daylight operations. Captain Tennant and Admiral Ramsay knew that further losses of shipping could not be tolerated. The previous day, Luftwaffe attacks had sunk four destroyers (one being French), four minesweepers and two passenger ships. Indeed, of the forty-one destroyers that had begun the evacuation, only nine were still operational. Tennant's mind was made up on watching six Stukas divebombing the old destroyer HMS *Worcester* and pounding her every five minutes without mercy. As she limped away from the harbour at a crippling ten knots with a horrifying casualty list of 350 dead and 400 wounded, Tennant told Major General Alexander, *'I'm sorry but that finishes it. I'm sending a signal to Ramsay to stop any more stuff coming in by day.'* From now on, evacuation would only take place under the cover of darkness. The decision was made all the easier by the belief that the coming night's operations were to be the last.

Early the next morning, Alexander embarked, but, before leaving, he toured the beaches calling out *'Is anyone there, is anyone there?'* In his account of his departure, he wrote that there was no reply. This seems true of British troops but a number of Frenchmen were still waiting for rescue. Certainly his comment to Eden later that afternoon that, *'We were not pressed, you know'*, would have been regarded with disdain by the French forces still desperately attempting to thwart the German advance into the town. Despite an admirable rearguard action by the French forces, the shrunken perimeter defences were crumbling. Bergues had fallen and the Germans, who were suffering considerable casualties, managed to enter Dunkirk's southern suburbs by the evening of 3 June. The Daily Intelligence report of 18 German Infantry Division recalls the last hours of the fighting:

'Until the morning of 4 June, the enemy showed by fierce artillery fire that it would resist at all costs. Then, very suddenly, the firing stopped. Major Chrobek was the first to understand what had happened. At dawn, the tired soldiers were loaded into trucks. Dunkirk lay lifeless. The streets were filled with burned automobiles and abandoned cars. Buildings on all sides were demolished. We asked ourselves, "Did the enemy save himself during the night?" Then our hearts leapt. Here was the sea – the sea!'

This extraordinary picture captures the different reactions of two advancing German soldiers, to the pleas of a wounded French counterpart.

With the large numbers of German troops filing into the town on the morning of 4 June, further resistance was useless. Operation Dynamo was

Germans entering the outskirts of Dunkirk.

officially ended by the Admiralty at 2.23pm. Inevitably not everyone did get out in time and some 30,000 troops, mostly the brave men of the 12ème DIM and the 68ème Division d'Infanterie, stood around awaiting imminent captivity.

Leading Signaller Alfred Cromwell was aboard HMS *Kellet*, the last ship out of the harbour area. Unfortunately, with the tide out and having already run aground once, the *Kellet* was forced to leave empty.

> *'We just couldn't get the gangway across to the pier. We were just too far out and no matter what we tried, we were unable to bring the ship near enough to the Mole. There were thousands of French troops waiting to get off. I felt very sad about it.'*

Another tragic twist to these remarkable nine days was the fate of Commander Jack Clouston, the man whose energy and leadership had led to such effective and speedy embarkations from the breakwater. The motor torpedo boat he was travelling in was hit and sunk by a Luftwaffe bomb and Clouston, exhausted by his efforts at Dunkirk, drowned. His legacy however lives on with the Mole's remarkable evacuation statistics. Indeed the miracle of Dunkirk occurred on this pier much more than it did on the beaches. Whilst the popular image of 'Dunkirk' is that of long lines of

The battle for Dunkirk is over and these exhausted German soldiers take time to relax in Place Jean Bart.

troops wading out to the small boats, the truth is that two and a half more times more soldiers were lifted off the Mole.

Date		From the Mole
27 May	...	7,669
28 May	...	11,874
29 May	...	33,558
30 May	...	24,311
31 May	...	45,072
1 June	...	47,081
2 June	...	19,561
3 June	...	24,876
4 June	...	25,553
Total	...	**239,555**

Wrecked fuel storage tanks to the west of Dunkirk still smoulder as German infantry stroll past.

Place Jean Bart where the Guards' bayonet charge finished.

What to See

The focal point to the town centre is the Place de Jean Bart, which is surrounded by restaurants and bars, as well as cheap accommodation. It was here that the Guards ended their bayonet charge. There is certainly plenty of evidence of heavy fighting around the Place, most notably the mass of bullet holes all around the base of the Church of Saint Eloi. Unusually, the steeple of this church is separated from the body by the Rue de Clemenceau. On the ground floor is the town's Tourist Information Centre, where you can get maps of the area and enquire as to the times for boat trips around the port and beaches (these vary according to the time of year).

On the westernmost point of Dunkirk's beaches is the Allied Forces memorial, which was built in 1962 and constructed with paving stones from the harbour quays. In many ways it is a rather soul-less monument, dedicated to 'the sailors, airmen and soldiers of the French and Allied

The battle scarred walls of Saint Eloi Church, still in evidence today.

Dunkirk Cemetery.

forces who sacrificed their lives in the Battle of Dunkirk.' It seems somewhat surprising that the momentous events of late May and early June 1940 were not thought worthy of something more impressive. Extending out towards the sea from the monument is the Eastern Mole, whose original wooden structure has now been replaced by concrete.

On the south-eastern side of the town, along the Route de Furnes, is the most impressive of all the memorials to those who died during the evacuation. To reach it, you need to park at the town cemetery and then walk some 400 metres along the main road. The names of the 4,516 British and Commonwealth servicemen whose graves are unknown are engraved on Portland stone panels on a series of large columns either side of a broad walk, forming an avenue which leads to a shrine. At the back of the shrine is a large engraved glass window depicting the deliverance of the BEF. Beside the memorial is a cemetery, where some 810 comrades who died in the Second World War lie. Of these, nine Navy, 651 Army, 141 Air Force, four Merchant Navy and five whose units could not be determined. Amongst those in the army are the graves of nine Canadian soldiers who died in September 1944 attempting to liberate the town. Amazingly, the German garrison at Dunkirk did not surrender until eight months later at the end of the war.

Memorial window.

CHAPTER SEVEN

OPERATION DYNAMO

At three minutes to seven o'clock on the evening of 26 May, the Admiralty sent out the message that 'Operation Dynamo' was to start. So began a nine day episode that was to become part of a nation's soul. The impossible was achieved with 338,226 servicemen safely returned by an armada numbering between 800-1200 vessels. The astonishing success of the evacuation was not lost on the men charged with its implementation. An Admiralty communiqué announced on the last day that:

'The most extensive and difficult combined operation in naval history has been carried out during the past week – when the full story can be told, it will surprise the world.'

The order to begin evacuation of troops from Dunkirk did not come as a complete surprise. Indeed contingency measures had begun some twelve days before when, on the nine o'clock news it was announced that:

'All owners of craft between 300 and 100 feet in length should send all particulars to the Admiralty within fourteen days, if they have not already been ordered or requisitioned'.

Neither the public nor the Germans, who regularly monitored the BBC, thought anything of it. The fact that people were given two weeks to do so hardly suggested urgency. Nevertheless, a small vessels pool was established and a number of men signed the form T124 by which they became subject to Royal Navy discipline for a period of one month in exchange for £3.

By 19 May the collapse of the Allied front in France had sufficiently alarmed the War Office for a discussion of *'the possible but unlikely evacuation of a very large force in hazardous circumstances'*. By 26 May a fleet comprising of forty destroyers, assorted 129 merchant and passenger ships waited in readiness.

Ramsay 'Architect of Dynamo'

The maze of galleries and tunnels hewn out of chalk by French prisoners during the Napoleonic Wars, and enlarged during the First World War, deep in the cliffs of Dover provided the basic headquarters of the whole operation. The Dynamo Room, from which the code name of the evacuation was taken, became the operation nerve centre. Beside it was the office of the man who was charged with the responsibility of ensuring the successful evacuation of the BEF, Vice Admiral Bertram Ramsay.

His job involved the organizing of the evacuation from its planning to its execution. As events were to prove, he was ideally suited to such a task.

Vice Admiral Bertram Ramsay

Nevertheless, that he was to have a nation's hopes and even future on his shoulders was somewhat surprising given that he had left the Navy in 1938. A brilliant career had at times been marred by his individual, innovative approach and ability to upset senior officers. As Chief-of-Staff to the Commander-in-Chief of the Home Fleet, Sir Roger Backhouse, he had felt deliberately excluded from all responsibility. Not a man to sit back and accept the situation philosophically, he resigned. However, as the shadows of war loomed, Ramsay was called back and appointed Flag Officer for Dover. The tasks involved in the job were familiar to him. They largely concerned defence against destroyer raids, the protection of cross-channel military traffic and the provision of army supply lines. Suddenly, in May 1940 at the age of just fifty-seven, he was ordered not to supply the army but to rescue it.

Ramsay was under no illusion as to the difficulty of the operation, as he explained in a brief note to his wife at the end of the first day:

> *'The situation is past belief, frightful. One wonders how the British public will take it when the full implications are realized. It's all too horrible to contemplate... I am directing one of the most difficult and hazardous operations ever conceived and, unless the good Lord is very kind, there will be many tragedies attached to it.'*

That the operation became a classic of improvisation was, to a large extent, due to Ramsay's energy and integrity. His efforts were recognized with a KCB soon after. However, his war by no means ended there and the superb organizational skills he had displayed in May/June 1940 were again tested when he played a key role in organizing the Royal Navy's part in the Normandy landings. Tragically, an air crash near Paris on 2 June 1945, in which he was killed prevented him witnessing the end of a war he had done so much to win.

An Inauspicious Start

A week before the evacuation the naval planners had assumed that the troops would be lifted off the three ports of Calais, Boulogne and Dunkirk. By 26 May only the latter remained open to them. To make matters worse, *Mona's Isle,* the first ship to make the 39-mile journey along the most direct route, came under heavy fire near the marker buoy at Calais on its return leg. The captain of the ship, Captain R. Duggan recalls:

> *'We were shelled from the shore by single guns and also by salvoes from shore batteries. Shells were flying all round us, the first salvo went over us, the second, astern of us. I thought the next salvo would hit us but fortunately it dropped short, right under our stern. The ship was riddled with shrapnel, mostly all on the boat and promenade decks. Then we were attacked from the air. A Junkers bomber made a power dive towards us and dropped five bombs, but he was off the mark too, I should say about 150 feet from us. All this while we were still being shelled, although we were getting out of range. The Junkers that bombed us was shot down and crashed into the water in front of us (no survivors). Then another Junkers attacked us, but before he reached us he was brought down in flames... the nerves of some of my men were badly shaken.'*

Mona's Isle eventually limped home with thirty-nine dead and sixty wounded. Other ships that attempted to pass along Route Z that night also received an unwelcome reception from the Germans who were using their air observation posts at Calais to excellent effect. The lesson was plain. An alternative route had to be found... and fast.

Two other possibilities existed but neither was satisfactory as both the Ruytingen and Zuydcoote passes (see map on page 64) were known to be impassable in heavy seas. Furthermore, Route X, the shorter of the two at 55 miles, had a French-laid minefield blocking its approach to Dunkirk. Ramsay therefore had little option but to use Route Y, a journey which at 87 miles was twice that of the direct passage. Even this was far from safe as magnetic mines littered the Zuydcoote pass and German artillery was coming alarmingly close to Nieuport, from where it could bombard the ships. Nevertheless, for the time being Route Y provided the only hope while North Sea minesweepers cleared the French mines along Route X.

Slowly, the armada began lifting the crowds of troops off the beaches. Few sailors had any idea of the seriousness of the situation or of the task that lay ahead of them. Thomas King, a rating aboard HMS *Sharpshooter,* remembers:

> *'It wasn't until we left Dover during the darkened hours that we were told that we were going to pick up an isolated bunch of soldiers from the*

Map 7
The Sea Routes

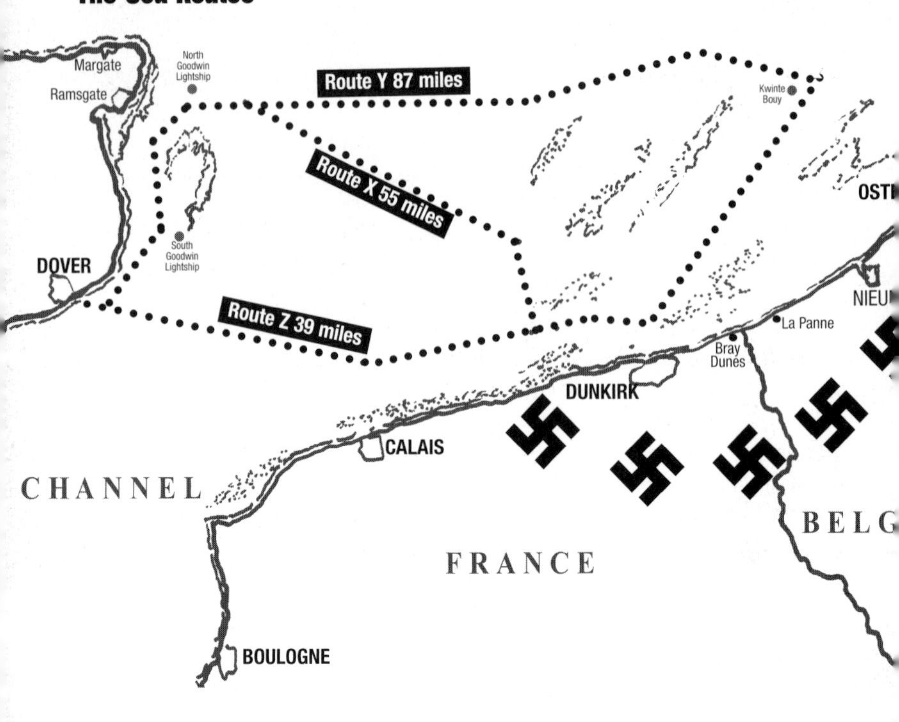

beach alongside Dunkirk. When we got near there our Captain hailed a ship coming out full of troops. "How many are there?", he called out, "Bloody thousands", came the reply. I shall always remember that.'

Soon the sailors were left in no doubt as to the critical state the BEF was in. Reginald Cannon, on board HMS *Fitzroy*, observed the soldiers' reactions:

'The emotion shown by many survivors was slightly embarrassing at times. Men hugging and kissing you in their relief but it was overlooked by the knowledge that we had rescued them, that they were alive, well and happy again and we were helping to get the boys back. There were also sad moments as one looked down on the deck at the rows of wounded. Some with eyes filled with tears and gratitude, others with no eyes at all. While many without arms, legs and other parts of their faces and bodies, lay motionless, staring from behind their bandages, in wonder, expectation and terror.'

There were many more wounded on the crammed hospital ships. John White, a doctor on *The Isle of Guernsey,* wrote a diary during this time:

'Down below, every cot is full and passageways crowded with stretchers. The dining saloon and smoke room are full of wounded and we gave up our cabins to the walking cases, eight or ten to a cabin. That familiar smell of sweat, dirt and disinfectants fills the atmosphere. The

Rescued. The faces of these men say it all.

Hospital ship *Isle of Guernsey*. During the evacuation she was repeatedly attacked both from the shore and the air.

wounded look exhausted, dirty and terribly ill and some of the badly wounded have had nothing done for them for days. A lot of these men will not make it, I fear.

There are some cases of shell-shock this time; terrified, crazed men whose brains have snapped after day and nights of strain, privation and terror. They were put below in one cabin under guard and given sedation injections. Eventually, when all seemed quiet, I went up to visit the wounded on the boat deck. To my horror and distress, eight had died, making a total of 12 on board. We are carrying nearly 1,000 wounded – and the ship was planned to take 250. There are wounded everywhere, even in the lifeboats. We do all we can sorting out the very ill and sending the ones that are not too bad down below to feed them. The ones too ill to move have been made comfortable with pillows and blankets on the deck. This is rough-and-ready doctoring with a vengeance, but a least they are on their way home.'

If the state of the troops was a shock to these unsuspecting sailors, so too was the tremendous opposition they received from enemy aircraft. Few ships escaped the attention of a rampant Luftwaffe hell bent on making the evacuation impossible. John Pearce was aboard HMS *Wolfhound*, an old destroyer, as it approached Dunkirk when:

'Out of the blue there was a peculiar screaming noise. We all looked at each other for a second before we realized it was Stuka bombers overhead. They made a terrible noise – that was half the terror. The ship immediately heeled over to port and the next we heard was a bomb screaming down. By that time you'd never seen such a panic in all your life. Rifles and kettles

Men being pulled from the water by the French destroyer *Branlebas.* Out of a ship's complement of approximately 800 men, crew and evacuated soldiers, 600 were rescued.

smashed against the walls, bodies were flying over and grabbing guard rails to stop them going over. Everybody was dashing to action stations with the alarm bell ringing simultaneously. It turned out three planes were attacking us and we eventually shot one down. This was our baptism of fire and a very frightening experience.'

The *Wolfhound* survived, but many ships were not so lucky. Philip Knight recalls the scene aboard the passenger

liner he was travelling on when it received a direct hit:

'It was complete and utter chaos. The crew hadn't time to lower the boats and some of the soldiers tried to take matters in their own hands but just didn't understand the launching procedure. She went down in three minutes and there were thousands of troops on board. I got onto the well deck just before it went under and went under with it. When I came to the

surface I saw my chaps shouting and gesturing from a Carley float... We saw one fellow tried to reach us but just before he got clear of the oil his hair caught on fire and he just went under.'

Many ships arriving and leaving the harbour were forced to pick up survivors from the sinking ships and water. If, like HMS *Kellet,* they were already full then it was up to the Captain's discretion as to how many more men could feasibly be crammed in. Alfred Cromwell was aboard *Kellet* when a nearby minesweeper suffered a direct hit:

'It literally broke her back. Kellet went alongside the disabled boat which was packed with men. We tried a controlled changeover but it was hopeless. The soldiers were going mad trying to get from one ship to the other. It could have been disastrous as we were in danger of being well and truly overloaded. Our crew tried to force soldiers back but it was hopeless. Eventually the skipper said, "Let them come and when we're ready we'll just shove off".'

It was heart-rending for all concerned seeing the bodies swimming around hopelessly attempting to attract the ship's attention to their plight. Where and when possible these men were picked up. Thomas King aboard HMS *Sharpshooter* particularly remembers one such case:

'We heard a shout and saw to our surprise a chappy sitting starkers on a laundry basket in the water. We got him on board, covered him up but he wasn't too bad for his ordeal!'

After a disappointing first couple of days, the embarkation rates began picking up considerably. By the end of the month a new armada was

A tug boat tows a fleet of small launches down the Thames.

Vessels of every shape and size were requisitioned and soon an armada of little ships were heading for the hell of Dunkirk.

appearing on the horizon to aid the evacuation effort further.

The 'Little Boats' Arrive

The Admiralty back in England had been far from complacent during the first few days of the evacuation. News that there was a desperate shortage of boats with shallow drafts only served to increase the urgency of those requisitioning and rounding up small craft. Men like Douglas Tough of Tough Brothers boatyard in Teddington were empowered to act as agents in their own area. Naval parties scoured the rivers, estuaries and creeks for suitable vessels as far north as The Wash. If the owners could not be contacted, their craft were taken away anyway. The majority of owners co-operated fully and some even took their boats to Sheerness, where they

A lifeboat is lowered to bring aboard a critically wounded man.

were met by a small Naval team under Admiral Taylor. Here vessels were serviced and provided with fuel, charter and a crew. The crew proved almost as difficult to obtain as the boat themselves. They were mostly made up of naval reservists, fishermen and others who had earlier put their names on form T124.

The evacuation was still a secret and these men, called up or sometimes volunteering on the spot, had no idea what they were about to be involved in. A number had very limited experience of the sea but, with red tape slashed, there was little time to question their credentials. Everyone who took part has their own story about how they became involved. Ronald Tomlinson, a trawler fisherman, recalls:

'We'd been fishing and, on arrival back at Ramsgate, we went to the cinema. Halfway through the film there was a newsflash asking anyone belonging to Ramsgate Trawlers to report to the Admiralty Office at once. When I arrived there, a man with lots of gold braid said, "Can you be ready by 5.00am with your crew?" He made no mention of Dunkirk or anything.'

Arthur Jocelyn, owner of a Thames barge that had never been out of the estuary, was equally unaware of what he was needed for:

'At 7.30am there was knocking at the door. It was my two brothers. One of them said, "Are you prepared to volunteer for a secret mission?" I replied, "Well, if you're going I'll go". "We've got to go down to the Royal Terrace and sign on at the naval command down there." When we got there I saw a mother in tears outside the office. She was in a terrible state. Unable to stop her son from volunteering, she cried, "He's too young – I've only got

him, his father's in France".'

Francis Codd was one of the firemen chosen to man the *Massey Shaw*, a London fireboat, which was sent across in the hope of bringing some of the fires in the port under control. He was not alone in volunteering for the job:

> *'We had an assembly at Blackfriars in which all eighty of our members were present. The Station Officer looking very solemn told us that he had received a message from Lambeth HQ stating the* Massey Shaw *was going to Dunkirk. We all gasped. He then told us that he wanted a crew. Every man stepped forward.'*

By the end of the month hundreds of boats were making their way across the channel. The work of requisitioning teams and the small vessels pool was now paying off. Vessels of every shape and size ranging from barges to fishing smacks, from cockle boats to yachts, headed towards the smoking port of Dunkirk. Many soldiers on the beaches recall being moved to tears by the sight of this vast flotilla of vessels that had come to save them. On 1 June news of the evacuation was broken to the public and countless other 'freelances' headed out from south coast ports such as Portsmouth, Eastbourne and Folkestone. Oliver Anderson on HMS *Sutton* recalls the scene at Dover as the destroyer returned with yet another load of troops:

> *'It was incredible really - like Piccadilly Circus, with ships ranging from destroyers to motorboats dashing away. We had difficulty threading our way through.'*

Many boats would have stood no chance of crossing the channel under

Transferring from one of the ferrying craft to a larger ship.

A hero's welcome, The London Fire Brigade's fire-float returns to the Thames after having made three trips to France and rescuing an estimated 600 plus men.

normal circumstances, but the sea was like a millpond. Many, like Victor Allen, could hardly believe their luck:

'The weather was unnatural. It just wasn't right and we all felt that a great power, God, was on our side. Around about that time in May and June it's often very choppy.'

Yet, despite these favourable conditions, some of the small boats never made it to Dunkirk. A number of those towed by larger vessels were simply unsuitable and had stanchions ripped off due to the pace they were being dragged along at. Furthermore, many motorboats had been out of service throughout the winter and engine failure was commonplace. Even without these problems, the crossing was treacherous enough for all vessels, large or small. The Luftwaffe had dropped large numbers of magnetic mines along the main routes during 29 and 30 May. Arthur Jocelyn, aboard his Thames barge, recalled one narrow escape:

'I was sitting on the cabin hatch when I looked outside and there, within three foot of the ship, was this round object. It was a mine. Only the wash from our barge kept it away. My heart went "thud, thud, thud". I suppose it was a magnetic mine and fortunately we were a little wooden barge.'

Other vessels were not so fortunate. The firefloat *Massey Shaw* had not yet reached the port when it saw a large French warship suddenly blow up about a mile away. Francis Codd was horrified at the damage these mines could do:

'We were there in five minutes. The ship had sunk completely and the

sea was full of screaming men. Only about forty were alive and all had injuries. We sailed into the middle of the survivors and tried to get some to grab our barge pole. We then dragged these injured men aboard. Many had broken legs and were cut and bleeding. It was an appalling sight and hearing the cries of these men is my most terrible memory of the war.'

The majority of troops were evacuated by larger vessels and not, as popular myth suggests, by the little boats which brought back less than thirty thousand. However, the small craft did invaluable work in ferrying the troops from the beaches to the troop carriers and destroyers that lay in deeper water some distance away. This operation was hazardous in itself as larger vessels understandably showed scant respect for these offloading boats tied up to them when threatened by sudden air attacks.

Many lives were lost during the evacuation. One of the most costly in human life was that of HMS *Wakeful* which was torpedoed by an E-Boat. Only those on the upper deck stood any chance of survival and all 600 below perished. A self-inflicted tragedy followed soon after when, in the darkness, HMS *Grafton* and HMS *Lydd* opened fire on the drifter *Comfort* which had stopped to pick up survivors. They mistakenly took it to be the offending E-Boat. The drifter stood no chance.

That such incidents occurred was regrettable but understandable. The men manning these vessels had been working around the clock. Many had lost count of the number of crossings their ships had made. Exhaustion affected everyone. Some sailors found the physical and emotional strains

Home at last!

too much for them. Constant stuka raids, fear of mines and torpedoes, the sight of helpless troops in the water and the burning wrecks of ships combined with a lack of sleep took its toll on the naval crews in the claustrophobic environs of a ship. Alfred Cromwell recalls:

'We had two stokers collapse in the stoke hold. They were severely burned having just collapsed absolutely exhausted... one telegraphist and one ordinary seaman were landed in straitjackets because they had gone absolutely mad through tension. The Chief ERA also went berserk – quite rightly too, because he was trying to get five minutes' rest when a cannon shell came through the side and grazed his shoulder.'

Fear spread like a disease on some ships. When a sub-lieutenant collapsed in fits and convulsions on the minesweeper HMS *Hebe,* twenty-seven members of the crew followed the next day with the same affliction. Morale completely collapsed on the destroyer HMS *Verity* and, returning from its fourth trip, twelve jumped ship. The destroyer was ordered to remain in Dover Harbour. Most, however, fought against the tiredness and horror to complete their awesome task with some ships making as many as nine journeys.

At 3.40 on 4 June the last British ship left Dunkirk. Operation Dynamo was over. That day Churchill addressed the House of Commons:

'The Royal Navy, with the willing help of countless merchant seamen and a host of volunteers, strained every nerve to embark the British and Allied troops... They had to operate upon a difficult coast, and often under adverse weather conditions and under an almost ceaseless hail of bombs and increasing concentrations of artillery fire. Nor were the seas themselves free from mines or torpedoes. It was in conditions such as these that our men carried on with little or no rest for days and nights, making trip after trip across the dangerous waters. The numbers they have brought back are the measure of their devotion and courage.'

Chapter Eight

ASSESSMENT – VICTORY OR DEFEAT?

'So long as the English tongue survives, the word Dunkirk will be spoken with reverence. In that harbour, such a hell on earth as never blazed before, at the end of a lost battle, the rags and blemishes that had hidden the soul of democracy fell away. There, beaten but unconquered, in shining splendour, she faced the enemy, this shining thing in the souls of free men, which Hitler cannot command. It is in the great tradition of democracy. It is a future. It is victory.'

New York Times, 1 June 1940

'For us Germans the word "Dunkirchen" will stand for all time for victory in the greatest battle of annihilation in history. But, for the British and French who were there, it will remind them for the rest of their lives of a defeat that was heavier than any army had ever suffered before.'

Der Adler, 5 June 1940

Few of the men in German Sixth Army, as they marched tentatively into the smoking ruins of Dunkirk on 4 June 1940, could have envisaged that the war would last another five years and that they would end up on the losing side. The British had capitulated and not even the remarkable evacuation could hide the scale of their defeat. Dishevelled, weary and weaponless, the men of the BEF arrived back in England. Britain's material losses during the campaign had been astounding, with its army's stores

Allied equipment gathered by the Germans for disposal as so much scrap for the Third Reich war effort. Taylor Library

British troops arriving in England pile up their rifles for overhauling before re-issue.

and equipment strewn around Northern France. The Navy too had paid a heavy price for its heroics. Six destroyers, five minesweepers, eight transport ships and a further two hundred vessels had been sunk with an equal number badly damaged.

British casualties amounted to 68,000, while French losses totalled around 290,000, with many more than that either missing or taken prisoner.

German casualties, on the other hand, amounted to 27,074 killed and 111,034 wounded. The statistics tell the story. Hitler had reason to be pleased with his forces, whose tactics, skill and fighting prowess had led to such a rout. His Order of the Day on 5 June stated:

'Soldiers of the West Front! Dunkirk has fallen... with it has ended the greatest battle in world history. Soldiers! My confidence in you knows no bounds. You have not disappointed me.'

On the other side of the Channel,

Churchill, too, was praising the efforts of his forces whilst warning that:

> *'We must be very careful not to assign to this the attributes of a victory. Wars are not won on evacuations'.*

Nevertheless the fact remained that, though Germany had achieved a total victory, Britain had not suffered a complete defeat. Churchill had predicted that 30,000 men could be lifted off, whilst Admiral Ramsay had hoped for 45,000. To everyone's astonishment the vast bulk of the army had been rescued and, while Britain still had an army, there was hope. The miracle of this deliverance lies in the number of extraordinary factors that made it possible. Gort's decision to ignore Churchill and the French commanders and head to the coast, the halt order, the weather, the survival of the Eastern Mole and the incredible determination of the Royal

British spirit in the face of defeat – a Tommy wearing a German helmet relieved from a member of an SS unit, is fed a tart by a member of the ATS.

Navy, all combined to save the BEF. General Guderian later reflected: *'What the future of the war would have been like if we had succeeded in taking the British Expeditionary Force prisoners at Dunkirk, is now impossible to guess.'*

It seems almost certain that, with a quarter of a million men in captivity, Churchill would have been left with little option but to bow to pressure for peace terms to be signed. Without a large amount of its professional army, it is hard to see how Britain could have recovered. In fact, Hitler never wished to enter into a war with Britain. He admired the country whose Empire he believed powerfully reinforced his ideas of racial domination, commenting that, *'To maintain their Empire they need a strong continental power at their side. Only Germany can be that power.'* After Dunkirk, however, he was stunned to find that his 'sensible peace arrangements' were continuously and categorically rejected. Even as late as 6 July Hitler insisted that the invasion of Britain would only be tried as a last resort 'If it cannot be made to sue for peace any other way'.

If the evacuation attempt had failed and Hitler's lenient peace treaty had been accepted, the outcome of the war might have been vastly different. With an extra forty divisions that were, due to Britain's continued hostility, required in Africa and on the Atlantic Wall, as well as with the 1,882 aircraft and their crews lost over Britain in the coming months, Operation Barbarossa could well have succeeded. Indeed, even without these forces the Germans managed to reach the outer defences of an evacuated Moscow by the first winter of the campaign, and that was after the fateful decision to delay the invasion of Russia until June 1941.

Significantly, Dunkirk aroused American sentiment. Epic accounts of the evacuation captured the public imagination and generated the first overt signs of popular and governmental support for Britain. The *Washington Evening Star,* the day after Dynamo's conclusion, argued that 'It is a matter of inestimable importance to our own security that we should instantly remove all restrictions on the rendering of realistic, material aid to the Allies'. If Dunkirk had failed, if Britain had signed peace terms or if it had shown any signs of breaking its spirit, then the USA would have been much less prepared to enter what was essentially a European war. As it was, the effects of Dunkirk were instantaneous and by mid-June some half a million rifles were on their way across the Atlantic. The whole episode and Britain's reaction following it, had proved the resolve of the nation, which Churchill's speech further highlighted when he promised that Britain would preserve 'the whole world from sinking into the abyss of a new Dark Age'.

This was vital as US Secretary of State Cordell Hull later commented, *'Had we any doubt of Britain's determination to keep on fighting we would not have taken steps to get material aid to her.'* If this is the case then one can be

The signing of the Armistice is over. Here French delegates, Admiral Le Luc, General Huntziger and Léon Noël, are escorted away by a German officer of the General Staff.

absolutely certain that the USA would not have later provided Communist Russia with vital supplies. Yet if Dunkirk was to help gain Britain one ally, it lost her another. At 8.50am on 22 June, France signed an armistice in the same wagon-lit at Rethondes, near Compiègne, where in November 1918 Marshal Foch had received the defeated German emissaries. Karl Heinz Mende summed up German feeling when he wrote home, *'The great battle in France is now ended. It lasted twenty-six years'.* The revenge was complete and, following General Huntziger's signature, the site was razed. A stunned French public could do little but bear witness to the speed of their country's collapse. France searched for a scapegoat. Dunkirk had left the French feeling abandoned and embittered towards their Entente partner and crude propaganda pouring out from Goebbel's bureau in Berlin further fuelled the flames of resentment. Stories of British troops forcing French soldiers out of boats and off the Mole abounded. The fact that over

How the German propaganda machine 'sold' the events at Dunkirk to the French people.

102,000 of the 123,000 French troops rescued were lifted off by British vessels was conveniently ignored.

Desperate attempts prior to the Armistice on 22 June were made to keep the Alliance together. Indeed on 16 June De Gaulle and Churchill had signed a 'Declaration of Union'. It did little, however, to disguise the mistrust and disillusionment that both nations now felt for each other. Britain had learnt the lesson that it would never again rely on other people's forces, and its post-war policy of building up an 'independent deterrent' of atomic weaponry reflected this. France, on the other hand, felt that Britain could not be relied upon militarily or economically if the going got tough. It was no coincidence that it was France, under De Gaulle, who prevailed upon Germany not to let Britain enter into the Common Market in the 1960s.

In June 1940 Britain stood alone. For some this was rather a relief. King George VI reflected such a sentiment in a letter to his mother Queen Mary on 27 June when he wrote: 'Personally I feel happier we have no allies to be polite to and to pamper'.

A number of generals, after their experiences in France, felt the same way. Churchillian grandiloquence played upon this 'Britain alone' theme:

> *'What has happened in France makes no difference to our actions and purpose. We have become the sole champions in arms to defend the world cause.'*

His rallying cries made an instant impression. Dunkirk had proved, with its much publicized civilian participation, that the war was more than a conflict between armies on the continent, the outcome of which the public were powerless to determine. The threat of invasion, along with the necessary myth of an army saved by the 'little boats', brought a nation together. A sense of involvement that had been lacking

A part of France would fight on under the banner of General De Gaulle.

A *Punch* cartoon invites the belief that Britain stands as an impregnable fortress against the might of Germany.

since the declaration of war now burst forth. Britain had sleep-walked into the war and it took the reverses in France and the evacuation to wake her from the complacency and over-confidence that existed prior to those events. Essentially, Dunkirk provided Britain with a second chance that had to be seized upon.

Churchill's leadership of the country had been doubted prior to the evacuation. Many, including Chamberlain, had favoured the less contentious Halifax. General Ironside believed that Churchill did not have 'the stability for guiding others'. John Colville, a junior member of the prime ministerial staff, observed that:

> *'The mere thought of Churchill as Prime Minister sends a cold chill down the spines of the staff at 10 Downing Street... His verbosity and restlessness made unnecessary work, prevented real planning and caused friction. Our feelings were widely shared in the Cabinet Office, the Treasury and throughout Whitehall.'*

After Dunkirk his leadership was never questioned. The eloquence of his patriotic and determined rhetoric captured the mood of the nation and inspired the citizens of Britain to unwavering defiance of the Nazi peril.

Preparations for the defence of the island were instantaneous. By mid-July over a million men had enrolled in the Local Defence Volunteers (LDV). Roadblocks and pillboxes sprang up everywhere, signposts were rearranged or removed, barbed wire and beach fortifications were laid. This was

Ready to repel the *Fallschirmjäger* and the *Waffen SS* should they attempt to set foot on British soil – 'Dads Army'.

total war. The country braced itself for imminent invasion. Copies of Hitler's peace offer made no impression on a people determined that, as Churchill put it:

'If the British Empire and its Commonwealth last a thousand years, men will say "This was their finest hour".'

By 16 July Hitler had lost patience. In Directive No 126 he stated,

'As England, in spite of the hopelessness of her position, has so far shown herself unwilling to come to any compromise, I have decided to begin to prepare for, and if necessary carry out, an invasion of Britain'.

But Hitler had, to borrow Chamberlain's earlier phrase, 'missed the bus'. It seems highly unlikely that Britain could have resisted a German invasion in early June. Churchill knew this and after his 'We shall fight them on the beaches...' speech, reportedly covered up the BBC microphone and said, 'but we've only got bottles to do so'. Certainly the BEF was in no position to fight. On their return, brigades existed as names only and the nation, dazed by recent events, had virtually no preparations in place. The recently created LDV units, with pitch forks and the odd shotgun, would have provided little more than a spirited but futile resistance. The depleted Navy, as well as the RAF, was Britain's only hope but the numerical supremacy of the Nazi forces provided Germany with a massive advantage. Hitler's decision to delay gave the country much-needed time to prepare. He refused to listen to his Generals. The only man who might have persuaded him otherwise was General Kurt Student, founder of Germany's airborne forces, who had worked out a plan for an airborne assault on Britain well before the invasion of France had begun. However, Student had been seriously wounded in Rotterdam. In the end, Operation Sea Lion was never attempted. Years later Student remained convinced that it could have been successful if it had taken place immediately after Dunkirk:

'Had we launched an airborne operation to occupy the ports where the BEF was disembarking, England's fate would have been sealed.'

General Kurt Student

An often-neglected consequence of the fighting leading up to Dunkirk was the effect it had on Hitler himself. His undeniably successful tactic of attacking through the Ardennes and his firm support of blitzkrieg tactics instilled a belief in him that as a military commander he was infallible. Hitler, the First World War Corporal, had proved that the caution of his Wehrmacht Generals was unfounded. Increasingly after Dunkirk, he made decisions that would have been best left to his commanders, and this was to have catastrophic effects during the Russian campaign.

A further consequence was that Dunkirk and the fall of France made him complacent. He had defeated the great warrior nation with ease and, with the same ill-founded optimism of Napoleon before him, he could see no reason why a similar lightning campaign in Russia would not have equal success. Such was his confidence that, as Britain awoke to the reality and necessity of 'total' war following Dunkirk, Hitler actually began

Beaten but still defiant.

demobilizing part of his own force and reduced his war productions.

All too often people just think of Dunkirk as the time when scores of patriotic citizens leapt into their small craft to aid their army in its hour of need. Certainly this occurred but the truth is that most of the small craft were in the hands of a wide assortment of Naval personnel. Rarely do people think about the defence of the soldiers on the perimeter and strongpoints, nor do they give enough credit to the Royal Navy and the larger vessels that were responsible for rescuing the massive majority of troops. Dunkirk became a necessary myth, but its importance in shaping the course of the Second World War has been vastly underestimated. Dunkirk was the beginning of the end for the Third Reich

BIBLIOGRAPHY

Barker, A.J. *Dunkirk - The Great Escape*, Dent, London, 1977
One of the best researched books on Dunkirk - interesting and informative.
Blaxland, G. *Destination Dunkirk*, William Kimber, London, 1973
Gives some excellent accounts of various fighting actions on the strongpoints and perimeter.
Brickhill, P. *Reach for the Sky*, Collins, London, 1954
The timeless biography of Douglas Bader.
Bryant, Sir A. *The Turn of the Tide: the Alanbrooke Diaries,* Collins, London, 1957
A brilliant insight into the mind of one of the Generals who shone at Dunkirk.
Chalmers, W.S. *Full Cycle, The Biography of Admiral Sir Bertram Ramsay,* Hodder & Stoughton, London, 1959
Churchill, W.S. *The Second World War Vol.II,* Cassell, London, 1964
Collier, R. *The Sands of Dunkirk,* Collins, London, 1961
Although its style is rather dated, this book is exhaustively researched and contains some interesting anecdotes.
Colville, J. *Man of Valour: The Life of Field Marshal The Viscount Gort,* Collins, London
Daniel, D.S. Hart *The Cap of Honour. The Story of the Gloucestershire Regiment 1694-1950,* Harrap, London, 1953
Particularly good account of the Glosters at Cassel.
Dean, C.G.T. *The Loyal Regiment 1919-53,* Mayflower Press, London, 1955
Divine, D. *The Nine Days of Dunkirk,* Faber & Faber, London, 1959
Fleming, P. *Operation Sea Lion,* Pan Books Ltd., London, 1987
A readable, although somewhat viscous, account of Hitler's invasion plans.
Forbes, P. & Nicholson N. *The Grenadier Guards in the War of 1939-1945,* Gale and Polden, London, 1949
Little more than an edited copy of the Battalion's War Diary.
Gelb, N. *Dunkirk - The Incredible Escape,* Michael Joseph, London, 1990
An excellent account of the nine days of the evacuation.
Gibson, G. *Enemy Coast Ahead,* Michael Joseph Ltd., London, 1946
Another well known aviation classic.
Gilbert, M. *Winston S. Churchill,* Volumes 5 & 6, Heinemann, London, 1976

Goebbels, J. *The Goebbels Diaries,* Ed. L. Lochner, 1949
Guderian, H. *Panzer Leader,* Michael Joseph, London, 1952
Harman, N. *Dunkirk - The Necessary Myth,* Hodder & Stoughton, London, 1990
Very readable, well informed account of events leading up to Dunkirk. It is largely written from the point of view of the Generals, rather than the 'ordinary soldier'.
Hamilton, N. *Monty – The Making of a General 1887-1942,* Hamish Hamilton, London, 1981
Hart, P. *At the Sharp End – From Le Paradis to Kohima,* Pen and Sword, Barnsley, 1998
An excellent regimental history of the Norfolks with many first-hand accounts. The account of the massacre at the strongpoint of Le Paradis is particularly harrowing.
Horrocks, Lt. Gen Sir B. *A Full Life,* Collins, London, 1960
Horne, A. *To Lose a Battle,* Penguin, London, 1988
This book covers much more than just Dunkirk. Superbly written, it provides an in-depth account of the fall of France, and is particularly good at analysing the characters involved in the struggle.
Howard, M. & Sparrow J. *The Coldstream Guards 1920-1946,* Oxford University Press, 1951
Keegan, J. *The Second World War,* Hutchinson, London, 1989
Kirby, H. & Walsh R. *The Seven VC's of Stonyhurst College,* THCL Books, Blackburn, 1987
Provides a good account of the action on the Bergues-Furnes canal which resulted in Ervine-Andrews' VC.
Langley, J.M. *Fight Another Day,* Collins, London, 1974
One of the most charming and amusing accounts of the fighting in France. Although wounded and, subsequently, captured defending the perimeter, Langley's war had by no means ended.
Lord, W. *The Miracle of Dunkirk,* Wordsworth, Hertfordshire, 1998
A gripping account. You do not need to be a military historian to enjoy this.
Lucas, J. *World War Two through German Eyes,* Arms and Armour Press Ltd., London, 1987
Masefield, J. *Nine Days of Wonder,* Heinemann, London, 1941
Montgomery, Field Marshal the Viscount. *Memoirs,* Collins, London, 1951
Nicolson, N. *The Life of Field Marshal Earl Alexander of Tunis,* Wiedenfeld & Nicolson, London, 1946
Plummer, R. *The Ships that Saved an Army,* Patrick Stephens Ltd.,

Northants, 1990
Anyone interested in maritime history who wants to know what ships were used during the evacuation should read it. A book for the naval equivalent of a trainspotter.
Ramsay, Admiral Sir Bertram. *Despatches,* Supplement to the *London Gazette*, 15 July, 1947
Shaw, F. & S. *We Remember Dunkirk,* Echo Press, Leicestershire, 1990
Woodward, D. *Ramsay at War,* Kimber, London, 1957
Young, Brigadier D. *Rommel,* Collins, London, 1950

UNPUBLISHED SOURCES

War Diary of the 1st and 2nd Battalions The Grenadier Guards.
War Diary of the 1st and 2nd Battalions The Coldstream Guards.
Recollections of Dunkirk by G.W. Jones and H.J. Mitchell.
Military Cross Dispatches for 2nd Lieutenant J.A.P. Jones.
'Grenadiers live up to their reputation'. *The War Illustrated,*
13 September, 1940.
'Amiens to Dunkirk - A Personal Impression', by General W.H. Nehring.
The Diaries of Rowland Young, 1940-1945.
Printed statements by Private H.J. Vaughan, Signaller A. Smythe, Lance Corporal F. Greenhough.
Private Diary of Captain H.C.W. Wilson.
'Withdrawal from Cassel' by Major S.H. Lynne Allen.
'A diary of the days spent in action in Belgium and France, 1940,' by 2nd Lieutenant J.P. Fane.
'A diary of events from 10 May – 1 June 1940', by Captain H.J. Lovett.
'A Company at Zuytpene,' by Major W.H. Percy-Hardman.
'An account of the holding of the Blockhouse, north of Cassel from
26 - 30 May 1940,' by Captain R.W. Cresswell.
'Cassel, May 1940,' by Lieutenant Colonel E.M.B. Gilmore.

INDEX